Letters to a Broken Church

Drawing on the personal experience of survivors of abuse and their allies, *Letters to a Broken Church* speaks directly into the existential abuse crisis facing the Church of England and other Christian denominations right now.

Its powerful message is that the structures, leadership, practices and culture of the Church must change radically to face up to the historic scale of abuse within its institutions at all levels.

The clear requirement for transparency and accountability after decades of evasion and denial is also highlighted in these essays, along with the need to make proper recompense to those whose lives have been impacted.

Contributors to *Letters to a Broken Church* include a serving bishop, a well-known newspaper columnist, several theologians and others from public life – but principally people in the shadows whose voices and experience as survivors have frequently been pushed aside, marginalised or silenced within the Church.

Here is a searingly honest, multi-voice call for action and redress that can no longer be ignored.

Janet Fife was one of the first women to be ordained in the Church of England. She is a writer and survivor and has a research degree in the pastoral care of survivors. She is disabled.

Gilo is a survivor, hymn-writer, and outsider theologian.

TRIGGER WARNING

Some of the material in this book may be disturbing for people who have experienced abuse directly or in terms of its impact on others. For those who may be seeking support, the MCSAS (Minister and Clergy Sexual Abuse Survivors) Freephone Helpline is: 08088 01 03 40.

Letters to a Broken Church

---

edited by Janet Fife
and Gilo

Speak Out
Survivors (SOS)

Ekklesia

First published in July 2019

Ekklesia
235 Shaftesbury Avenue
London
WC2H 8EP
www.ekklesia.co.uk

All biblical quotations are from the New Revised Standard Version, unless
otherwise stated

Views expressed in this publication are the responsibility of the individual
contributors and do not necessarily represent the views of the publishers. We
have made every effort to ensure that they are fair comment

Production and design: Bob Carling (www.carling.org.uk)

Managing Editor: Simon Barrow

ISBN: 978-0-9932942-6-6

A Catalogue record for this book is available from the British Library.

Contents

Publisher's Preface

It is an honour for Ekklesia Publishing to produce this book on behalf of the editors, the very diverse contributors, and a network of collaborators who we have called, informally, Speak Out Survivors (SOS). This publication has taken much longer to emerge than we hoped or anticipated, but its message is as topical as ever.

That acronym 'SOS' is appropriate too, because the abuse crisis within the Church of England, the churches as a whole, and many other institutions across society is indeed an emergency and a vast wound.

There is an entirely justified sense of frustration, anger and betrayal within and toward church communities in particular. This is because, as *Letters to a Broken Church* illustrates vividly and painfully, the culture of avoidance and denial concerning the nature and extent of the abuse crisis continues to this day, especially among many in positions of ecclesiastical leadership.

The Christian church supposedly witnesses to a God whose love changes lives, transcends tribal boundaries and puts the poorest and most vulnerable – not least the violated and abused – first. In practice, however, church bodies often behave in ways that flatly contradict this message, even rendering bureaucratic lack of concern, evasion and refusal of accountability in a language of piety that only adds insult to deep, life-long injury.

In that sense this book is a call to repentance (a call to turn round and head in a completely new direction) issued not *by* the Church, but *to* it – from those who have suffered and by those who stand in solidarity.

A failure to change radically and fundamentally in relation to the messages in this book so can mean nothing less than that the Church itself has 'lost the plot' – in this case, the transformative narrative of the Gospel itself. The stakes are that high.

Simon Barrow
Director
Ekklesia

Introduction

This book gathers together thoughts from two dozen victims and survivors, commentators, theologians, lawyers, Church figures, General Synod members, and others. The views held by each are not necessarily the views of all – but together they offer a wide range of perspectives on the Church of England's abuse crisis. We thank all the contributors who have given their time generously without any remuneration. Thanks too to all the supporters of this project, listed at the back of the book, who made publication possible. Each anonymous donation is listed as a separate 'Anonymous' entry – to honour each person's contribution.

This book will not the be the last word on this subject, nor necessarily the best. Much more can be said, and many more stories visited. We are conscious of important absences due to restricted space between the covers of a book. Abuse in Church of England children's homes, abuse of military cadets by Padres, clergy complicity and unease involving pressure and cover-up. To name just a few of the notable absences.

We hope there will be plenty more books both by individuals and collectives. There *needs* to be many more. And the huge body of material on the IICSA (Independent Inquiry into Child Sexual Abuse) website is likely to become source for many academic studies in the future. It charts the story of a church in breakage and a gospel in collapse. The Church of England is in crisis, and will only redeem the astonishing mess it has made of its response to all this by full, honest and transparent ownership of that crisis. Ownership will come about through the speaking of truth to power.

So let plenty more commentary on all this history hasten transformation of structures and internal cultures, so that the Church of England can deal justly and honestly with all survivors and come to terms with its own brokenness. We hope that in time it can mend – both itself, but far more importantly, the lives of so many it has harmed and continues to harm.

If you buy this book for yourself or for another, please be aware that some of it may be triggering for any who are themselves victims and survivors of abuse.

Any profits from this book and the fundraising that enabled it, after costs have been covered, will go to support the work of MACSAS (Minister and Clergy Sexual Abuse Survivors), and towards the cost of a possible conference and related activity.

Gilo

Janet Fife

July 2019

Chapter 1

The Deacon's Tale

Anne

In my ordination photos I look radiant. I'd completed my three years of training and moved far away from my family and friends, but I was looking forward to getting started in my new ministry. I would be working in a big city centre church with several clergy, and my role would be to look after the congregation pastorally. The decision to ordain women to the priesthood was still several years away, and female deacons were few; my clergy colleagues were all male.

My training incumbent (my new boss) and his wife were very welcoming. He (we'll call him Fred) was dynamic, with a charismatic personality and a vision for the church's work and outreach that had me enthused. Once I'd started working for him, however, another side emerged. Fred could be abrasive and unfair in his dealings with people. Before long I had witnessed some very unpleasant episodes of bullying, and some bouts of explosive temper. In addition, what I at first took for friendliness began to take on a sexualised tone. I was uncomfortable with it but didn't know how to react – I was a very new curate and a woman in a man's world, and out of my depth.

When I received a memo suggesting (ostensibly as a joke) that the way for a woman to get promoted was to sleep with the boss, I wrote a spirited reply. One evening Fred and I were in the churchyard after a service when I felt his hands come round me from behind. I froze in shock as he held me close against him. It was dark but there were people about, and after a while he moved away.

After that I tried to avoid being alone with Fred, but it was impossible. It's inevitable that a curate spends a lot of time with their training incumbent, especially in the first year.

The tension of the situation grew, especially as I began to realise just how ruthless Fred could be. HIs motto was: "People will go for your jugular, so you've got to get in first." Additionally, two others of my male colleagues felt free to correct me or tell me off if I got something wrong, even when (as often occurred) I had never been told how they wanted it done. It was a highly dysfunctional team. Although we all said morning and evening prayer together daily, there was hardly ever a time when we were all on speaking terms. There were always at least two members of the team at outs with each other. I found it difficult to share the Eucharist, and the peace, in those circumstances. It was so false.

One day after matins, several of us headed for the church office to pick up our post. I was there first, and Fred followed me in and pinched my bottom. This time I protested indignantly, but Fred was unabashed. I was a bad sport, he said, and the parish worker who had preceded me hadn't minded. He turned for confirmation to a fellow curate who had just come in, and he agreed. Clearly I wasn't going to be supported by my colleagues.

By this time I was on anti-depressants. My doctor, knowing my boss and working environment, was not surprised. He treated other staff from the same church.

I had learned to be very afraid of Fred. I had seen him set out to destroy one person after another – and he usually succeeded. There would be a lull after the latest target became ill or left (or both), as if some compulsion in Fred had been satisfied. After a few weeks, though, he would start in on someone else. Slander, bullying, aggression, false accusations – all were weapons in his armoury.

There were things I enjoyed about my job and I liked and valued many of the congregation, but my situation was intolerable. I was working more than 80 hours a week, but Fred felt I still wasn't doing enough. When I was in bed with a chest infection he phoned and gave me a rocket for not attending a staff dinner. By now I was getting the full Fred treatment; he made comments from the pulpit which were clearly aimed at me and criticised me to others. I learned that the situation was being discussed by the congregation in home groups. At one time Fred instructed the church treasurer to withhold my expenses for several months, apparently just to punish me. I was not long out of college, and by the time I was several hundred pounds out of pocket I was quite desperate. I had to plead for the money.

One day Fred said to me, "We treat people well when they leave. You should try it." I decided to see the bishop and ask him to move me to another parish. He knew Fred's reputation as a bully and a womaniser, so I thought there was a good chance he would agree to my moving. Bishop John had told all the curates he would be available within 24 hours if we needed to see him, so I expected an early appointment. I was taken aback when his secretary told me the bishop couldn't see me in less than six weeks. Eventually, however, I did find myself in Bishop John's study, telling him my tale of bullying and sexual harassment. He heard me out. Then he said, 'I'm not going to move you. And I will tell Fred you've been to see me about it.' I felt as though I'd been kicked in the stomach. I can still feel that sense of utter dismay and despair that hit me that day. Not only was the bishop refusing to help, but he was making things infinitely worse by betraying my confidence and telling my abuser I'd reported him.

I didn't know what to do. The only solution seemed to be to leave the ministry altogether. I had such a strong sense of vocation, though, that I couldn't really see that as an option. Besides, I'd given up my flat and my job to train, and didn't know where I could go or what I could do if I left my curacy and the accommodation that went with it.

Eventually it was another diocese that came to my rescue. A friend arranged an appointment with the women's ministry adviser there, and she facilitated my move. I was still within my training period, but they well knew Fred's reputation and were very sympathetic. I am still grateful for the help they gave me; had it not been for them I think I would have become so ill that I couldn't work at all. My old diocese didn't make it easy, though. Bishop John said to me when he heard of my move, 'If you leave now, the scent of failure will follow you throughout your ministry.' He later sent me a letter saying he'd written to my new bishop and new incumbent objecting to my move. That was vindictive; he was determined I wouldn't have a smooth start.

Three months after I left my first post, Fred's promotion was announced. In the Church's eyes, his sexually predatory and generally aggressive behaviour did not unfit him for high office. Several years after that, the bishop also moved, to a bigger and 'more important' diocese. I have recently heard of at least two more cases where this same bishop refused to act on allegations of abuse.

In the decades I have worked for, and in, the Church of England I have seen this pattern many times over. Behaviour which I would consider un-Christlike and unprofessional seems not only a bar to preferment – it's almost as if it's considered a qualification. There have been a few good bishops and archdeacons, of course, and I have been very grateful for them. It's clear, however, that those who make a fuss about the bad behaviour of predators and bullies cannot expect a 'good' post. The Church closes its ranks against whistleblowers. Fortunately for me, since that early experience I have always preferred to work on the margins and had no desire for high office, so have been free to speak out. But I have watched good priests and fine leaders passed over, evidently because they rocked the boat. The whole Church is poorer for this – especially when those who do get promoted are the ones who leave every nettle ungrasped. The Church's vineyard has become a field of nettles.

It's only recently that I have been able to come to terms with the events of my first curacy. They have affected the whole of my ordained ministry. I have never since been able to cope with the Daily Office; the thought makes me shudder. I have never again felt that I could trust my superiors in the Church; never again felt that it was my 'mother Church'. At the same time, I have partly blamed myself for what happened. Did I unintentionally 'lead Fred on'? Did I allow him to think I would welcome his advances?

Those feelings of fear and guilt needed to be brought out into the open, so I sought and received counselling. Now I know how unreasonable it was that I should feel in any way responsible. The man was known to be unsafe with women. As a clergy wife commented, 'Fred wears his sexuality on his sleeve.' I had heard tales of his groping other women; of staring down the cleavage of a woman in the congregation, remarking, 'You look a million dollars.' He told me himself of visiting a single female member of the choir at night and plying her with gin.

The year before last I reported Fred's abuse to the National Safeguarding Team (NST), saying, "Everyone knew what he was like with women." After some investigation an NST officer commented to me, "You were right. Everyone knew." As far as I know, no disciplinary action has been taken.

I am telling my story now in the hope other women will feel free to speak about their experiences. I cannot be the only woman priest who has had difficulties of this sort, but I have never heard the subject talked of. While in secular society female survivors telling their stories greatly outnumber males, in the Church women have been largely silent, and absent from protests. I surmise there are two reasons for this.

Firstly, other women have learned – as I and male survivors have – that speaking out does the abuser no harm, but may well damage the complainant in the eyes of the Church. There are so many ways whistleblowers can be punished: difficulty in changing jobs if you're labelled a 'troublemaker'; lack of diocesan co-operation when applying for grants and funding; harsh ministerial reviews.

Second, the position of women in the Church has been precarious and hard-won. While loud voices are claiming we are not truly priests;

while we are still. In a 'period of reception' of women's ordination; while supporters still have barely acknowledged doubts about our suitability for leadership; what woman wants to present herself as a victim? The last thing we need is to give the doubters another reason to say 'no' to us. We have had to be strong.

The full story of women in the church still needs to be told. Someday it will be told. But for now, I hope more female victims of abuse will be empowered to say #MeToo. Only then can they and the Church journey on towards wholeness.

*'**Anne**' is an Anglican priest.*

Chapter 2

Can a Price be Put on a Soul?

Rupert Bursell

The Anglican Church recognises two very different forms of confession: general confession, said collectively as part of a service; and private, person-to-priest confession (called 'auricular confession'). The latter is practised almost entirely, if not exclusively, by Anglo-Catholics. Apparently in the Roman Catholic Church the practice of auricular confession, which was previously widespread, has decreased dramatically since the recent horrific revelations of child abuse, particularly in Ireland and North America. However, there are no statistics to show whether there has been a similar decline in the Anglican Church.

Nevertheless, it is seems fair to assume that the secrecy surrounding auricular confession may attract to confession those who are abusive as a private means towards salving their consciences, whilst in other cases an abusive priest may find a secret space in which to indulge in his abuse. However, such a suggestion should in no way be taken to imply that more than a very small number of those who take part in auricular confession may act in such a manner.

The secrecy surrounding auricular confession is due to what is called 'the seal of the confessional' which was without doubt part of the pre-Reformation canon law as it applied in England. It was reflected after the Reformation in the proviso to Canon 113 of what are called the Canons Ecclesiastical 1603, and in The Book of Common Prayer 1662. The proviso states:

> Provided always, that if any man confess his secret and hidden sins to the minister for the unburthening of his conscience, and to receive spiritual consolation and ease of mind from him, we do not in any way bind the said Minister by this our Constitution, but do straitly charge and admonish him, that he do not at any time reveal and make known to any person whatsoever, any crime or offence so committed to his trust and secrecy (except they be such crimes as by the Law of this Realm, his own life may be called into question for concealing the same) under penalty of irregularity.

The meaning of this proviso (which still remains in force) is not entirely clear but it is often appealed to by those who claim that there is a legal privilege against a priest disclosing any matter divulged to him in a formal, private confession.

The penalty fixed by the proviso to Canon 113 for breach of this confidentiality is that of "irregularity", that is, "deprivation [from office], accompanied by incapacity for taking any benefice whatever, while under its observation" (see Blunt The Book of Church Law (9th ed., 1891) at page 176).

However, since the passing of the Ecclesiastical Jurisdiction Measure 1963 a censure of deprivation can only be passed by the relevant Church court if the offence of which a priest is found guilty is one "involving matter of doctrine, ritual or ceremonial" and the court is satisfied that the priest has already been "admonished on a previous occasion in respect of another offence of the same or substantially the same nature"; otherwise it cannot pass a censure more severe than a monition (that is, an order to do or to refrain from doing a specified act) or a rebuke (see section 49(3)). Nowadays, too, under the 1963 Measure the offending cleric is not deposed from Holy Orders unless the diocesan bishop makes a further order of deposition (see sections 50 & 51). It follows that, if a breach of the seal of the confession would in law be an offence involving a matter of doctrine, no penalty of deprivation could be imposed for a first offence (whatever the proviso may say).

On the other hand, if it does not involve a matter of doctrine, the nearest equivalent penalty in the Clergy Discipline Measure 2003 is that of "prohibition for life", namely, "prohibition without limit of time from exercising any of the functions of his Orders" (see section 24(1)(a)). In this case there is no possibility that the cleric can be deposed from his or her orders, a result that would be likely to be extremely offensive to many survivors of sexual abuse.

In spite of pre-Reformation canon law and the subsequent proviso there is nonetheless considerable doubt whether any appeal to the seal of the confessional would be accepted as valid by a non-ecclesiastical court (whether criminal or civil); even if it were to be accepted as valid, the Terrorism Act 2002 already provides legal inroads into the scope of the seal (see sections 19(1), 20 & 38B). What is more, as Anglican church law is (unlike Roman Catholic canon law) part of the general law of England, Church law cannot be at variance with the general law. Yet that is by no means the only hurdle that anyone wishing to rely on the seal of the confessional has to overcome. This is because there is no legal definition in any Church law books as to what in law constitutes a 'confession' and, before there can be any such reliance, it would first be necessary to define in law precisely what a 'confession' is.

The 1603 proviso, of course, speaks of a penitent wishing to unburden his conscience as well as a wish to receive "spiritual consolation and ease of mind", presumably through absolution. The other relevant passages are to be found in the *Book of Common Prayer:* that is, in the exhortation in the Order for Holy Communion and also in a rubric in the Order for the Visitation of the Sick. The former of these speaks not only of confession "with full purpose of amendment of life" but also of the need for reconciliation and "being ready to make restitution and satisfaction", while the latter speaks of receiving:

> the benefit of absolution, together with ghostly counsel and advice, to the quieting of [the penitent's] conscience, and avoiding all scruple and doubtfulness.

It follows that any confession that is argued to attract the seal of the confessional should have a number of separate components: a wish to unburden the penitent's conscience and to receive spiritual consolation; an unreserved intention to amend his life; a readiness to make restitution and satisfaction; and, lastly, the granting of absolution. These, for example, logically rule out a 'confession' entered into as a joke or as a manipulation of the priest by the purported 'penitent'. Yet, in spite of this, many Anglo-Catholics argue that the seal of the confessional takes effect immediately anyone commences on an apparent confession. If that were, indeed, the case, the seal would even cover a prank made with no intention whatsoever of unburdening the soul or making any amendment of life. Yet for those Anglo-Catholics to accept otherwise would be to open the door to the need to consider whether there is a true confession at all and, therefore, to whether the seal does in fact apply. In fact it would seem more logical to accept that each of the above elements is required to be fulfilled before there is a confession which should be recognised as such by the law. Indeed, it should be for the courts to decide whether there is a confession that should be legally recognised rather than for the decision to be made by the individual priest concerned.

This matters. Anglo-Catholics accept that a person confessing sexual abuse of a child should himself report the fact of his abuse to the social services or the police; this is the consequence of the requirement of a readiness to make "restitution and satisfaction". In fact, the priest should offer to accompany the abuser to the authorities and, unless and until the penitent makes such a restitution, any absolution should be withheld. A failure -certainly any continuing failure – to make such restitution also seems to undermine (or, at least, to bring into question) any suggestion that the 'penitent' really has an unreserved intention to amend his life.

Without restitution and without absolution the question must be whether there is any confession at all to which a claimed seal can attach. The matter has become so convoluted that, for example, in the diocese of Canterbury, although the clergy are told in its Diocesan Child and Adult Protection Guidelines (April 2015) that "Canon law constrains a priest from disclosing details of any crime or offence which is revealed in the course of formal confession", those hearing confessions are nonetheless enjoined first to make the following statement to those coming to confession:

> If you touch on any matter in your confession that raises a concern about the wellbeing or safeguarding of another person or yourself, I am duty bound to pass that information on the relevant agencies, which means that I am unable to keep such information confidential.

Either there is a binding constraint (in which case what is the point of the subsequent enjoinder?) or there is not. That apart, the enjoinder (if followed) leaves any abused person open to continued abuse and the (otherwise) penitent person without the benefit of absolution.

The argument that the seal of the confessional becomes binding from the moment that any person purports to commence a confession (however defined), and even though no absolution has been given, is based at least by some Anglo-Catholics on the argument that, if there is no seal, the abuse would be less likely to be confessed and therefore the possibility of the abuser being counselled by the priest to report to social services or to the police would be removed.

Nevertheless, as the abuser might still refuse or neglect to report the matter, any present or future victim of his abuse would thereby continue to be left unprotected.

Alternatively, some Anglo-Catholics argue that the possibility of the abuser's repentance (and consequent salvation) should always be left open and that this possibility might be jeopardised by the priest's reporting the matter to the authorities. Such an argument, however, seems to be based on a fallacy; namely, that God's forgiveness must be channelled only through the vehicle of the confessional. Nevertheless, of greater concern is the corollary that without such reporting the survivors of the abuse, and any future victims, are left open to the continued depredations of the abuser. Is that a price that those innocent persons should be forced (unasked) to pay? If so, that would seem to be the price paid by them for the mere possibility that the actual abuser may at some time in the future enter into a proper repentance.

I cannot believe that a just and merciful God would expect such a dreadful price from any person, whether a child or no. What, too, of an abuser admitting to his abuse after another (innocent) person has already been convicted and sentenced for that very abuse? Why should that innocent person pay such a price? Does God ever demand such an unwitting price, especially as the mere *possibility* of the abuser's self-reporting may never be fulfilled?

The Rev Canon Rupert Bursell QC is an Anglican priest and abuse survivor. He has served as a judge and as chancellor of several dioceses. In 2018 he was awarded the Canterbury Cross, "for his contribution to the understanding and application of ecclesiastical law in the Church of England."

Chapter 3

Keeping Secrets – The Church of England and Shame

Miryam Clough

As a young woman exploring a vocation to ordained ministry in the Anglican Church in New Zealand in the 1980s, I sought the support and guidance of clergy. While the overt sexism and prejudice I was confronted with by some was not unexpected, I was surprised to find, among those priests who were supportive of my vocation, several who were also unboundaried and predatory.

For the three decades that followed, I took responsibility for scenarios and relationships that had confounded me in my twenties. It must have been my fault. Now, at 56, with daughters the age I was then, I look back on those men and wonder what on earth they were doing. Where was the guidance and mentoring that I was looking for? Where was their sense of pastoral responsibility, their professionalism? Where, indeed, was their responsibility to their wives and families? Why, when I was avoiding a married parish priest more than twice my age (I was 21) who was threatening to kill himself if I didn't run off with him, was my vocation doubted when I withdrew from his congregation? Why, when I sought support to deal with certain situations, was I advised not to rock the boat? Why, when even bishops knew what I was contending with, did they not act?

Now that I am the age that one of those priests was then, I watch my daughters and their peers with sheer admiration as they strive to follow their respective vocations, and I find it inconceivable that any of those clergy acted as they did.

These are tales of broken boundaries. Of deeply unprofessional behaviour by men much older than I was, who should have known better. In my twenties, there was a brief sexual assault by an unmarried priest I was seeing who had trouble understanding the word 'no'. Much later there was a sustained period (over some years) of emotional abuse with some episodes of physical violence. This was my experience of some Anglican clergy on both sides of the globe.

Even now, I find myself squirming internally as I reveal this information. I still feel responsible. I still fear reprisals and blame. I still experience shame. I was an adult and not without resources, yet these experiences shook me up profoundly and my mental health was, at times, compromised. How it must feel to someone who endured clergy abuse in childhood or adolescence, I can only imagine.

It takes profound courage to tell our shame stories. There can be catharsis and healing in the telling, providing those receiving our stories respond with empathy and without judgement. Additionally, shame stories are a catalyst for change. Unless these stories are told, unless we are open about the flawed state of the Church and the exploitative nature of some of its clergy, abuse will go on. Abuse thrives on secrecy and secrecy is dependent upon shame. Shame is, I believe, the mechanism that has perpetuated a culture of abuse within an institutional Christianity that is already susceptible due to its dualistic, masculinist theology. If the Church is to truly address and redress this abusive culture it is imperative that it develops an understanding of shame and that it acknowledges the gendered power structures that underpin clerical abuse.

Shame is the affect and emotion that says 'I am bad, I am flawed, there is something wrong with me'. Unlike guilt, which triggers the realisation 'I have done something bad or wrong, I've made a mistake', prompting us to put things right, shame says 'I am the mistake'. In the grip of shame, we lose agency. We struggle to recover our equilibrium. We are afraid and unable to speak out. We want to hide, to avoid exposure. We might wish the ground would swallow us up.

Physiologically, shame sets up a stress response pushing us first into fight or flight and, if it continues, into freeze. A state of hypoarousal is characteristic of shame, as it is of the affects disgust and sadness. The switch in autonomic nervous system activity attendant to shame causes a reduction in tone in the body, neck and facial muscles which accounts for the characteristic head hang, slumped posture, downturned mouth and averted gaze. The blush of shame is the result of reduced sympathetic vasoconstrictor tone and corresponding vasodilation. We get physically stuck in shame. If the shame is prolonged, it gets wired in. Our neural pathways change. Shame is debilitating.

Some people are more susceptible to shame than others. Shame-prone individuals are more convenient targets for abusers. Shamed individuals do not readily speak out. We shoulder the blame, taking responsibility for the abuse, believing we are inherently bad and somehow deserving of it. We fear exposure and rejection. Shame ensures silence. Silence allows abuse to continue. Shame is a powerful mechanism for control.

Additionally, shame is isolating and a form of social pain, causing relationships to break down and individuals to feel alone, vulnerable, powerless and disaffected. Isolation itself is a powerful means of social control. Shame is also linked with scapegoating, as uncomfortable issues are pushed outside of the community and heaped onto 'troublesome' individuals or groups to make the dominant group feel better or safer. By isolating abused individuals and silencing them through shame, abusers are free to continue abusing.

A complication of abuse is that abusers are also locked into shame. Psychiatrist Donald Nathanson's Compass of Shame is helpful here. The four poles of the compass are attack self, attack other, avoidance and withdrawal.

In two of these shame aspects we take the shame on, becoming overwhelmed by self-disgust. In attack self, we 'beat ourselves up', sometimes resorting to physical self-harm, taking responsibility for the wrongdoing of others, believing it is somehow our fault. In withdrawal, we are disempowered by shame, we take ourselves away and may slip into depression. Shame is closely linked with eating disorders, personality disorders, addiction, self-harm, depression and suicide.

In the other two aspects, we attempt to push shame away by deflecting it onto others. In attack other, we resort to aggression and violence against the object of our shame. Sociologist Thomas Scheff and James Gilligan, a psychiatrist who worked for many years with violent offenders, assert that shame and the attempt to regain self-esteem underpin every act of violence, even to the extent of contributing to international conflict. Neuroscientist Allan Schore has identified the physiological mechanisms that move us from shame to rage, giving weight to this perspective. In avoidance, we retreat into narcissism and denial, bolstering ourselves up and projecting our shame onto others. Borderline personality disorder sits at one end of the shame spectrum, narcissistic personality disorder at the other.

The former manifestations of shame ensure that victims of abuse do not speak out. The latter see abusers blaming victims, compounding the abuse and failing to take responsibility for their actions. And so, the cycle of abuse and shame is perpetuated. Those survivors of clergy abuse who have sought support or redress from the Church will know that these various manifestations of shame also operate at institutional levels. A shame-bound institution will seek to cover up, will resist exposure, will be incapacitated by shame and unable to put things right. A shame-bound institution may resort to attack other and narcissistic avoidance, projecting its shame by victim blaming and derogation.

Individuals who find themselves targets for abusive clergy are likely to be vulnerable in other ways. They may be very young, they may be suffering and seeking support, they may be placing a lot of trust in the priest who becomes their abuser. That priest, viewed as morally righteous, trustworthy, and even impervious to sin is in the perfect position to abuse. Traditional Christian theology and doctrine have fostered a culture where clergy are placed on pedestals and seen to do no wrong. We do not see abusive priests coming, and when we encounter them, they are difficult to challenge. The unboundaried and abusive priests I crossed paths with were experienced, credible, respected and valued by many of their parishioners and students. They all had their good points. However, they lacked professionalism, abused their power and one was physically violent, yet they were protected (and certainly not challenged) by their male colleagues. I continue to be surprised by what some got away with.

By failing to act, the Church provides shelter, not to the vulnerable or wounded – to those it claims to minister to – but to its hierarchy. What this tells us is that clerical abuse is a systemic issue that requires a systemic response. As Philip Zimbardo noted in his TED talk *The Psychology of Evil* (2008), the question to ask is not "who are the bad apples responsible?" but "what is the situation and where is the power in the system?"

"If you want to change the person", Zimbardo says, "you've got to change the situation. If you want to change the situation, you've got to know where the power is in the system". To address clerical abuse, the Church needs to reconsider its theology, teaching and hierarchical structure. Additionally, it needs to bring its professional training, standards and procedures into the twenty-first century.

Arguably, two thousand years of masculinist theological constructs that elevate the masculine, especially the male priesthood, to a transcendent, spiritual realm and align sex, the body and the feminine with sin and death, have facilitated a culture where the (male) priesthood is powerful and untouchable. Within this discourse, women, children, gay men and non-binary individuals are easily disrespected and repeatedly silenced. In recent decades, plenty of feminist and queer theologians have proposed alternative theological models that seek to address this ludicrous imbalance and foster inclusivity. It is high time this material moved into the mainstream. A theological and doctrinal shift is long overdue.

Shame is maladaptive. A shamed Church seeks to hide its failings and may reject or blame those it has wronged. Guilt, conversely, is an adaptive emotion that motivates the desire for reparation where there has been wrongdoing and seeks the restoration of fractured relationships. A guilty Church will acknowledge its collective and historical wrongdoing and act to put things right.

It will take a confident and committed Church to respond well to those who have survived abuse at the hands of its clergy. That response, I believe, requires a rethinking of some fundamental theology, a willingness to atone, and an understanding of the workings of shame and secrecy that have facilitated a culture of abuse that has hitherto been swept under the carpet. It also requires a shift in ecclesiology to replace clerical power and privilege with clerical responsibility and service. This volume presents a call to the Church of England to atone, to make amends, to put things right.

Dr Miryam Clough *is the author of* Shame, the Church, and the Regulation of Female Sexuality *(Routledge, 2017).*

Chapter 4

Unstoried: Men's Abuse of Women and Girls

Natalie Collins

Jo Kind was the Rev Tom Walker's personal assistant from 1989 to 1991. He explained to her that the medication he was taking for a heart condition caused a problem with his libido and that his doctor had advised him to be without his clothes as much as possible, and so he would work naked in the office. During her time working for him, she reports that he would walk around naked in various states of arousal. She eventually reported his behaviour to the Church in 2008 but it took until 2015 for Mr Walker to be "rebuked" by the Church of England disciplinary process.

After taking civil action against the diocese, the parish church where she had worked for Walker awarded Jo Kind £40,000 (before legal costs) but did not admit liability. The diocese required Jo to sign a non-disclosure agreement before it would allow her to read the redacted report. In 2018, Jo was interviewed about the NDA and told her story to Channel 4 News. Jo did not break the NDA in speaking to the press, since she did not divulge the report's contents. A bishop had told Jo in 2011 that it would be "ungodly" to speak to the media, but she said to Channel 4 interviewer Cathy Newman:

I have no fear of being ungodly in that way because I have asked for 10 years for the Church to speak up about this and they haven't, and I thought that they would with this review. And I thought that was the right and proper way to do it. I went through all the Church procedures and I think I've reached the end of the procedures and so am speaking to you now.

In 2014, the Rev Simon Marsh was arrested on suspicion of rape and sexual assault. A teenage girl had begun attending his church, as she wanted to deepen her faith. Allegedly, Marsh began grooming this girl in January 2011 and began raping her in 2012. According to the girl, his behaviour became "increasingly coercive, aggressive and controlling". On one occasion "he got angry after she spilt coffee and 'insisted' she perform a sex act on him". Although the Crown Prosecution Service did not find enough evidence for the case to proceed to trial, the Archdeacon of Macclesfield brought the case to a Church disciplinary tribunal. Marsh was found guilty, removed from office and prohibited from ever again exercising ministerial functions in the Church of England.

Timothy Storey was employed as a youth worker by an Anglican church in London. In 2002 he raped a 17-year-old girl from within the congregation. She describes his abuse in this way: "He ground me down and treated me like a piece of meat... I felt like a blow-up doll. He once said to me, 'You are not worth wasting a condom on.'" Storey groomed another teenage girl via Facebook. He gave her alcohol, took her back to his home and raped her twice. She described him as "more influential than God". Both girls individually reported Storey to the church. The first was told by the priest that the Church needed to "look after" Timothy Storey and that they had to think about his "welfare and needs". The second girl was told that a safeguarding officer was "dealing" with her disclosure. Storey then began training as an ordinand. In 2015, Timothy Storey was convicted of grooming hundreds of children via Facebook. After seeing news reports of Storey's conviction, both girls reported his perpetration of rape to the police. He was convicted and sentenced to fifteen years in prison. While the Diocese of London acknowledged failing the girls, no disciplinary proceedings were enacted.

These are some of the very few church leaders whose crimes make it into the public consciousness. There are thousands of others whose violence and abuse remains hidden. In two out of three of these cases, the Church hierarchy colluded with the offender, minimised his offences and prioritised his feelings and needs over those of the victims. Too often this is still the case.

A decade ago I began working to address domestic abuse, contracted by a local authority to run groups for women and support the training of professionals. I continually met professionals who had a Christian faith and they encouraged me to resource the Christian community. Ten years later, and countless Christian women have courageously shared with me the ways their Christian husbands have abused them. Some of their husbands are priests.

When a woman is abused by a partner, his abuse will take many different forms. He may isolate her from family and friends, degrade and humiliate her, exhaust her, demand her servitude, control the finances, use their children (if they have any) as a weapon against her, interfere with contraception to impregnate her, use technology to spy on her or control her, have affairs, minimise his behaviour, convince her she's going mad (this is known as gaslighting). He may rape her or reject her, be indifferent to her, lie to her, and as a Christian he may use the Bible to justify his behaviour and demand her acceptance of it. "The Bible tells you to submit." "You have to forgive me." "If you were a better wife, I wouldn't have to hurt you."

When someone is doing these things and he is a priest, there are additional layers to the abuse. When he tells her no one will believe her, she knows it's true; he puts on that collar and everyone presumes he is closer to God. When his calling requires her to give up her job and move to theological college, she can't explain that her job was the one thing that ensured she had some autonomy. When he punches and kicks her in the stomach and she miscarries her baby, she cannot tell anyone because if he loses his job, she and her other two children will lose their home. When he has an affair with the churchwarden, she can't divorce him; she's now fifty-three and has spent most of her adult life supporting his ministry. She has no recent work experience to get a job so as to afford somewhere to live. All her friends are part of the church and they think her husband is a fantastic leader. His mission programme has brought so many new families to the church. If she leaves him, it's not only her marriage and family that falls apart, but so does the congregation she has spent decades investing in and loving. His calling to partner with Jesus in bringing life in all its fullness to his flock is the very thing that gives him such power and control over his wife and children.

Whether in Christian circles or not, one of the enduring realities of abuse is the way that those subjected to abuse are blamed. The abuser's intentions and the impact of his choices are whitewashed. It is a curious thing; the Christian faith is infused with grace, but we can only handle sin if we diminish it and make it manageable and palatable.

Abusers are whitewashed and victims are blamed for the same reasons. Alongside all sorts of socialising factors, there is an enduring issue of psychological safety. Human beings need an ordered world; to feel confident that they can identify who is dangerous and who is safe. This is particularly the case for those in authority (most especially in church authority). We all want to live in a world where we are able to make character judgments that are accurate. When someone is a domestic abuser they rarely abuse anyone other than their partner and children. In fact, they want others to be their allies, and so will work hard to ensure they are liked and respected. This allows them to maintain control. If the abuser's partner or children disclose his abuse, the person receiving that disclosure is faced with an existential crisis:

"Do I accept that this woman is telling me the truth, imploding all my presumptions about who is safe and who is dangerous? If so, how do I continue to live in a world where those I know to be good people are abusive and dangerous? I won't be able to keep those I care about safe, maybe those I care about could even be abusers?!"

And so, in that moment, they shift the narrative... She must be exaggerating. It can't be abuse. They're having marital troubles. Let's get them some marriage counselling. I'll have a word with him. She's overly emotional. Best get her some therapy as she's clearly got self-esteem issues.

Similarly, victim blaming is also about psychological safety. If the victim is not at fault then there's nothing she could have done to protect herself. Therefore, there is nothing any of us can do to ensure that we will not be raped or abused. And worse still, our daughter may be raped or abused, there is nothing she (or we) can do to guarantee no one will hurt her. And so, we blame those who are abused, because if we can identify what they did wrong we can prevent our daughters being abused. Then we can breathe a sigh of relief and know they are safe.

The girls who were abused by Simon Marsh and Timothy Storey were not at fault. Neither was Jo Kind, or the women who have shared their stories with me. Yet the Church is rarely a sanctuary to them. It compounds their pain and colludes with the abuser. The Bible becomes a weapon, pushing them to submit, forgive, and eschew divorce. For women who are abused there is an additional burden of being relegated as the "weaker sex" in a biblical tradition which has erased us (Junia), turned men raping us into our adultery (Bathsheba), our sexual exploitation into a fairy tale (Esther), our leadership into the punishment of men's failure (Deborah), and our apostleship into a minor part (Mary Magdalene). Purity culture leaves us sexless while simultaneously Proverbs warns of women aggressively enticing men. And this is before we consider the wider Western narratives of misogyny in media, culture, and politics.

There is much to be done. We need a seismic shift in both Church culture and across the Church's theology; not solely in her handling of abuse allegations, but in the Church's view of women and girls.

It is no surprise that people are often under the misapprehension that males are the majority victims of abuse in the Church when the Church treats women and girls so badly. Theologian Riet Bons Storm explains that women's experiences often remain "unstoried", because they never find a person or a space that is safe enough for them to construct their experiences into either a psychological or a verbal narrative. Let us commit to become safe people and build communities where women feel safe enough to tell us their stories, even if that requires us to dismantle our constructs of safety as we realise how helpless we are to prevent abuse. And as we do that, we will perhaps discover more of the God who chose to enter into that helplessness with us.

Natalie Collins *is a Gender Justice Specialist working to enable individuals and organisations to prevent and respond to male violence against women.*

Chapter 5

Recognising Dangerous Safeguarding Practices

Ian Elliott

In 2016, I was asked to undertake a critical case review for the Church of England. Prior to undertaking this task, I had very little knowledge of or contact with the Church as I am not a member. I live in Northern Ireland and am a practising member of the Presbyterian Church of Ireland. However, my expectation was that the Church had a sincere interest in learning from the mistakes that had been made in previous years and that, at the highest level, there existed a desire to ensure that these errors were not repeated. Two years later, I no longer hold that view.

On the contrary, my belief today is entirely different and has been shaped by what I have observed over the intervening years. The Church of England has invested much energy and considerable resources in ensuring that significant changes were made. However, when it comes to holding people accountable for bad practice, nothing much has been done. Those who have committed abuse or failed to report it, have not been challenged even when they have brought the Church into disrepute and, in some cases, are thought to have committed crimes. In short, the Church has learned to tolerate and accept dangerous safeguarding practices, believing that all that is needed is the creation of a safeguarding policy framework and a raft of new posts which carry the label "safeguarding", and that these will be sufficient to keep the wolf pack away from the door of the Church. They will not achieve that objective.

I spent six years working with the Irish Catholic Church trying to set in place a safeguarding culture that confronted and challenged the dangerous, secretive, and shortsighted practices of the past. When the new culture started to gain ground, those who engaged in the cover up of abuse learned to expect challenge both from within the Church and from outside. Bishops lost their positions and were forced to resign. Survivors of clerical abuse could no longer be silenced by the cheque book and became focused on an entirely new phenomenon, holding their perpetrators and those who covered for them, to account. The power of the hierarchy diminished and those who had appeared to be impregnable suddenly felt the cold wind of change.

It was a turbulent time and it required a high degree of personal commitment to see it through and not run away. However, change did take place resulting in a letter from Pope Benedict XIII to the Irish Catholic Church expressing his distress at what the mismanagement of clerical abuse had given rise to. Several bishops were forced to resign because of the new scrutiny and public criticism.

When looking at the situation that exists within the Church of England today, I am struck by the similarity with the Irish Catholic Church of 2007. Dangerous safeguarding practices are evident and appear to be woven into the very fabric of the hierarchy who maintain a commitment to not seeing what most other reasonable people in society can appreciate, namely that the Church does not hold clerical offenders or those who cover for them to account.

What enraged the strongly Catholic population of Ireland so much was the complete disregard of the hierarchy for the suffering that was caused to victims by known abusive priests. Bishops ignored survivors of abuse and often sought to hide and protect those who had caused harm. Offending priests were moved from parish to parish or sent to questionable treatment centres, run by the Church, before being brought back into ministry. For years, these dangerous practices were commonplace and nobody believed they could be changed.

When questioned, the Church misled and misrepresented the situation as a way of trying to keep the lid on. Eventually, the dangerous practice of cover up collapsed, and the house of cards started to fall. Catholic Ireland was transformed to such an extent that the Irish Prime Minister, Enda Kenny, who is himself a committed Catholic and frequent mass attender, delivered a blistering attack in the Irish Parliament on the hierarchy, which resonates even today. The Irish ambassador to the Holy See was withdrawn just to further emphasise the point.

It happened in Ireland to the established Church of the state and it has every chance of happening to the Church of England if they continue as they are doing. When I refer to dangerous safeguarding practices, specifically I would highlight the failure to pass on to the police or the social services allegations of abuse made against a member of the clergy. There has also been a failure to maintain appropriate records of relevant conversations with survivors or others who report alleged abuse, including the destruction of documentation which relates to those matters without reporting the incidents. All of these have occurred within the Church of England as can be evidenced by the statements made by those who were called before the Independent Inquiry into Child Sexual Abuse sitting in London. As reported, they appear to be established patterns of behaviour for many.

The case that I reviewed and reported on in 2016, provided further examples of dangerous practices. What was unusual about that case was that the survivor spoke of his abuse to many people, some in very senior positions, some of whom confirmed that the conversations took place, but they took no action to pass the information on to the appropriate authorities. They just received the allegations but did nothing with them. Others who the survivor says he remembers speaking to, are unable to recall the conversations that were reported to me. However, many did remember, and I do regard the statements made by the survivor to me as entirely credible.

One of my recommendations for the Review that I undertook was the creation of an independent safeguarding authority that would oversee the practice that took place within the Church. Quite simply, I regard this now as a necessity as I have come to believe that without it, nothing will change. When I submitted the report, I was told that the recommendations had all been accepted and they would be implemented as a priority. There is no evidence that this is the case. In fact, there is much to suggest that they have now been set aside and replaced by a new set of priorities, none of which address the major difficulty that the Church has at this time, and that is a lack of ability to recognise and remove dangerous safeguarding practices.

It pains me to have to state that I view the Church of England as being on the brink of a major crisis that will threaten its very structure. There is no support in English society for child abuse or for those who seek to cover it up, no matter who they are. People in authority in the Church who see themselves as being impregnable, would do well to look to the experiences of others in positions of power in Churches elsewhere in the world. They could learn from what happened to those people when it was revealed that they had covered up abuse or helped hide abusers. Archbishop Philip Wilson in Adelaide and Cardinal George Pell in Sydney are just two examples from the Australian Catholic Church.

Bishops John Magee and John McAreavey from the Irish Catholic

Church are others.

There is a growing list of prelates who now find themselves being held to account in a way that few would have considered possible a short time ago.

When you look at the revelations that have already been shared through the IICSA inquiry in London about the appalling practices of the Church of England in recent years, it would seem inevitable that more will come out. A tipping point will be reached where society will wake up to the fact that all is not well within the Church of England. Can Church leaders be trusted to report honestly on what is known to have happened? Enough has already been uncovered to make a negative response to that question. Files have been burnt. Allegations received and ignored. Disclosures made and not acted on. What more is needed to reach a point where it must be recognised that independent scrutiny of practice is not an optional extra, but a necessity if the Church is to avoid terminal decline?

I would argue for the adoption of a new culture within the Church which seeks to welcome those who have been harmed. Rather than deny and deflect criticism, learn from mistakes and change. Introduce mandatory reporting within the Church and seek to lead the rest of society. Hold offenders accountable and make it unacceptable to not act on allegations of abuse when they are received. All these would help, but for them to be adopted there must be a willingness to change. There is little evidence at present that this exists. For that reason, I remain pessimistic that the dangerous safeguarding practices that I have highlighted will end before the inevitable major crisis forces change to occur.

***Ian Elliott** is an independent safeguarding consultant that has worked across five continents and with many Churches. He is a professional social worker with over forty years of experience gained within statutory child protection services and within voluntary bodies. He was the director for the NSPCC in Northern Ireland and was appointed the inaugural Chief Executive Officer for the National Board for Safeguarding Children in the Irish Catholic Church, a post he occupied for six years. He has delivered many keynote addresses to International Conferences, written articles, and contributed to professional books focusing on the protection of children. He is a committed Christian and since establishing his consultancy in 2013 (www.ianelliottsafeguarding.com), has concentrated on*

supporting faith communities and Churches responding to the discovery of abuse. He has written review reports that have led to change in highly contentious situations. He is married with three children, five grandchildren, and lives in Northern Ireland.

Chapter 6

Dear Justin and John...

Janet Fife

This piece was first published as the blog 'A Survivor's Response to the Archbishops' Pastoral Letter', on 25 March 2018.

I'm writing in response to your 'Pastoral Letter'. And, since Archbishop Justin has called for an end to clericalism and deference, I'm going to call you Justin and John. I know you'll be happy with that.

So, Justin and John, I thought you might want to know how I, as a survivor, feel about your letter. And I know you'll pay careful attention, because you've said you want to listen to survivors.

But first, let me talk a bit about the IICSA hearings. In the last three weeks I've been on an eventful personal journey. The first week I was emotionally chewed up: the evidence recalled to me many of the awful experiences I've had over my nearly 40 years in the Church of England. The second week I began to realise that at last powerful people were being called to account and some of the rottenness was being exposed. Frankly, John and Justin, I enjoyed seeing those bishops wriggle under questioning from two women who were much younger than them. The tables were turned and it did me a power of good.

During the third week I felt empowered. By then I was getting things in perspective. You see, being a survivor of childhood sexual abuse, and also one of the first women to be ordained, has been really tough. So often the treatment I've had from the Church has replayed those old scripts. And often I'd felt bad because somehow I didn't seem able to pick up the rules of the game, didn't have the formula for being taken seriously by the hierarchy. What was wrong with me? Now I know it wasn't me who was wrong, it was the dreadful system and so many of the people at the top. (Not all of them, thank God, but too often the good were outweighed by the bad.) Now I'm glad I never learned those rules. They were, and are, rotten rules to play by. As Justin said last week, we need to learn from what has happened and make massive changes. I was quite encouraged. I actually had some hope, Justin, that you meant it.

And now, John and Justin, to your letter. Oh dear. I'm afraid you could hardly have got it more wrong. So let me give you some friendly advice. Let's start with topping and tailing. If you're going to address us all as 'Sisters and Brothers in Christ', don't finish with 'The Most Rev and Rt Hon'. It's just not brotherly. It looks like showing off. It certainly doesn't look like the shame Justin said he felt. If you really wanted an end to deference and clericalism you'd have signed off 'Justin and John'. We know who you are.

Next, if you want to send out something called a pastoral letter, make it pastoral. Asking for prayer for all those involved in the IICSA hearings and in safeguarding isn't enough. You can't just pass on to what good work is being done without saying what you are actually going to do for those affected by the hearings. What practical steps have you taken to help survivors, for instance? In case you can't think of anything you could and should do now, here are some suggestions:

1. When someone writes to you personally with an allegation of abuse or harassment, as I did last November, answer them. Your chaplain or secretary can draft the letter, but sign it yourself. At least make sure they actually get a reply. I haven't had one, and it's 133 days now. Not that I'm counting.

2. Announce that you are setting aside funds for counselling for those who have made allegations of abuse. All I was offered, in a phone call from a member of the safeguarding team, was a meeting with a female priest. I'm a woman priest, I know dozens of women priests. It takes a skilful and trained counsellor to help a survivor of abuse. Invest some money into putting things right.

3. We've all heard accounts of abuse taking place in church settings, as part of worship and prayer. You speak of all the services of Holy Week as if everything will go on as usual. If it does, you will rob us of that glimmer of hope we had when Justin seemed to struggle with tears about the abuse people have suffered in our Church. So, announce that you are stepping back from your role in all the Holy Week observations and ceremonies. Tell us you will instead spend the week visiting survivors and listening to our stories. You could ask ordained survivors to take your place in some of those services. That would demonstrate your respect for them, your admiration of their courage and honesty. Give them some of the outward show of dignity you would usually enjoy.

Another point: if you're going to start a pastoral letter with a biblical quotation, make it an appropriate one. The passage which came to my mind when I read your letter was another saying of Jesus:

So when you are offering your gift at the altar, if you remember that your brother or sister has something against you, leave your gift there before the altar and go; first be reconciled to your brother or sister, and then come and offer your gift (Matthew 5.23–24).

We have just spent three weeks finding out how much is justly held against the leaders of our Church. The debt is huge, but you can at least make a start. John, you need to work on being reconciled with Matthew Ineson before you next attend church. Justin, what about making amends to Gilo for those 17 unanswered letters? But only if you take Jesus seriously, of course.

Finally, I'd like to say, in my most pastoral manner, that neither of you seems good at responding appropriately to people who've been on the receiving end of the bad stuff that happens in religious organisations. So here's another suggestion. When you need to write a letter like the one we've just had, or to make a statement, run it past a survivor first. Most of us don't want you to look uncaring and incompetent, we really don't. We can help you to write sensitively, to respond appropriately, to offer assistance that will actually make a difference. Many of us have years of experience working with other survivors; researching; struggling with the theological and spiritual implications of being abused. Some of us can even contribute liturgical material you might find useful. We survivors offer a resource for the Church that you need badly. Don't continue to despise it.

Well, as far as I'm concerned this has cleared the air nicely. I do hope you've found my suggestions helpful; there are plenty more I can think of but I reckon this is enough for now. Feel free to ask my advice any time. It's funny what a difference it makes, being able to call you Justin and John. Almost as if I really were your equal in Christ.

Yours sincerely,
Janet Fife

Janet Fife was one of the first women to be ordained in the Church of England. She is a writer and survivor and has a research degree in the pastoral care of survivors. She is disabled

Chapter 7

The Gospel, Victims, and *Common Worship*

Janet Fife

What has the Gospel got to offer victims of abuse? What is 'good news' for those whose most urgent problem is not their own sin, but the damage done by someone else's sin against them?

A survivor attending a Church of England *Common Worship* Holy Communion service (and many parishes offer nothing else) might well conclude that Christianity cannot help them. The focus is entirely on sin and forgiveness, and the work of Jesus presented almost solely as saving us from our sins. The theme runs through the service from the penitential material at the beginning to the prayers before the distribution of the consecrated elements, and is sometimes repeated in the post-communion collect.

Undoubtedly salvation from sin is a key theme both in the Bible and in Christianity generally. I would argue, however, that to narrow the gospel down just to forgiveness from sin as the Church is currently doing, is to seriously distort it. I'll illustrate this by looking at two examples from *Common Worship*.

The first is the introduction to the confession in Holy Communion Order One:

> God so loved the world
> that he gave his only Son Jesus Christ
> to save us from our sins,
> to be our advocate in heaven,
> and to bring us to eternal life.

Contrast it with John 3.16, which it quotes:

> For God so loved the world that he gave his only Son, so that everyone who believes in him may not perish but may have eternal life.

Verse 17 continues:

> Indeed, God did not send the Son into the world to condemn the world, but in order that the world might be saved through him.

The original in John offers relief from the fear of death, with the implication of a new quality of life now, and freedom from condemnation "to those who believe". The invitation to confession more specifically names Jesus's mission as "to save us from our sins", with "to bring us to eternal life" second, and as a delayed prospect. It also introduces the idea of Jesus as our "advocate" – lawyer – in heaven. The whole mood of the passage has changed from freedom and relief, provided for us by God's overwhelming love, to apprehension of appearing in the dock in a cosmic courtroom with God as Judge – a daunting prospect, even with Christ as our barrister.

Moreover, rather than approaching our advocate directly, we are supposed to rely on an intermediary – the priest – to dispense absolution. The idea of an intermediary other than Christ is foreign to this passage from John, and scarcely present in the New Testament.

Our second example is the options given for prayer before the distribution of Holy Communion. Both distort the lesson to be gained from the tale of the Syrophoenician widow in Matthew chapter 15 and Mark chapter 7. The point of the story is that God's grace is so abundant that it's available to all – "even the dogs eat the crumbs that fall from their master's table". Even Syrophoenician women are 'worthy' to eat the crumbs – how much more so the children of the household! And yet, after confession, absolution, sermon, declaring our faith, exchanging the Peace and all – we are supposed to say we are less worthy than dogs. This is hardly Good News, especially for those downtrodden and lacking confidence.

The virtues of *Common Worship* are that there is supplementary material, and that it allows freedom to borrow from external liturgical sources, especially during the ante-communion. Few clergy make the most of this freedom, however. The core of the liturgy used in most parishes shows a very limited understanding of the mission of Jesus. Understandably, then, even regular worshippers can assume that Jesus was born and died solely so that our sins can be forgiven.

Contrast this assumption with Jesus' own declaration of his mission in Luke 4.18–19:

> The Spirit of the Lord is upon me,
> because he has anointed me
> to bring good news to the poor.
> He has sent me to proclaim release to the captives
> and recovery of sight to the blind,
> to let the oppressed go free,
> to proclaim the year of the Lord's favour.

There is nothing in this passage about sin. Jesus speaks here of being sent to the poor, the prisoners, the blind, and the oppressed; and he speaks not of forgiving them but of healing them and setting them free.

Likewise, the Sermon on the Mount, the core of Jesus's teaching, begins with words of blessing for the poor (Luke) or poor in spirit (Matthew); the meek; the persecuted; mourners; and the hungry (Luke; Matthew has "those who hunger and thirst for righteousness"). It is clear that Jesus is concerned for those who suffer, whether physically or emotionally, and meeting their needs.

Jesus challenged some people regarding their sin, especially religious leaders. However, he healed and delivered many to whom he does not seem to have mentioned sin. He resisted the others' attempts to reduce everything to a question of sin and guilt, and frequently criticised religious leaders for laying heavy burdens on 'ordinary' people and the poor.

The concept of salvation itself has been narrowed to a focus on the forgiveness of sin. The principal Hebrew term for salvation (*yesa'*) means 'to make room for' or 'to bring into a spacious environment'. It connotes freedom from things which restrict or limit. It is the word from which the name 'Jesus' is derived. The Greek term *sozein* originally meant 'to deliver from danger' or 'to make safe'. In both Hebrew and Greek the word used for 'salvation' meant safety, deliverance from danger, and freedom from restriction.

Sin is one of the things which threatens and restricts us, and saving us from sin was certainly part of Jesus' purpose. But other things also threaten and restrict us, and particularly the survivor of sexual abuse: fear, shame, despair, self-loathing, poor decision-making. Children and young people who are abused are not given the right conditions for growth, and their development into psychologically healthy adults is restricted. A true sense of self must be given space to develop. For them maturing into Christ will mean not sacrificing self, as much traditional teaching demands, but learning who they are and what they want. Psychological limitations such as the inability to set boundaries, trust one's own perceptions, or seek to have one's needs met are properly a part of the work of salvation. As Kathleen Fischer commented, "the movement of God in our lives emerges as we come to know our deepest selves" (*Women at the Well: Feminist Perspectives on Spiritual Direction,* p. 114).

We seldom see this wider picture of salvation reflected in our liturgy, which is the 'shop window' of our Church and both reflects and moulds our theology and spirituality. The seasonal material, including collects and Bible readings, does draw on themes such as events in the life of Jesus and the doctrine of the Trinity, but these are still set within a framework which is almost exclusively about the sins and need for forgiveness of the worshipper.

Imagine the effect of this skewed emphasis on those who come to church hurting physically and emotionally, frightened, with no sense of self respect, and never having had a chance to discover who they really are. They are faced almost immediately with a prayer saying God knows all our secrets, and are then required to search their own hearts and minds for the things they have done wrong.

For an individual in such a condition the confession can be a further abasement. Imagine if, instead, they were greeted with: 'Jesus said, the Spirit of the Lord is upon me, because he has anointed me to bring good news to the poor ... to let the oppressed go free...', and the rest of the liturgy took its theme from that. It would be liberating not only for sexual abuse survivors, but for many others: the poor, the depressed, the sick, and those struggling with all kinds of problems. And I suspect that is exactly why our liturgy wasn't put together like that.

It is the powerful who get to frame the liturgy, especially in an established Church like ours. Our liturgy of course has its roots in the Roman Catholic Church, but from the time of Constantine the Catholic Church too was very close to the centres of power and influenced by them. Put simply, there are two reasons why the ruling classes would want the Church to focus on the sins of worshippers and their need for forgiveness, rather than Christ's subversive claims to free the oppressed and bless the poor.

The first, and perhaps most obvious, is that they don't want their hold on power threatened. It suits them that the common people should know their place and be without a sense of their own dignity. Much better to keep them preoccupied with their own sins and failings, their own need to be forgiven, than to remind them that in God's Kingdom the last shall be first and the first shall be last. If, in addition, access to the grace of God is via a priest, rather than directly, that is a powerful tool for keeping people in their place.

The less obvious reason for an overemphasis on sin and forgiveness is a lack of imagination on the part of those who frame the liturgy. Those who are in positions of power in the Church – in Britain, traditionally, educated and affluent white men – have generally had little experience of oppression or powerlessness. It is easy to see, therefore, why their theology should emphasise personal responsibility. That is a healthy corrective for the powerful, who can maintain the illusion that they are always able to exercise choice. For many people the experience of being powerless and having limited choices is more real; but if all your associates are of the dominant class you may not realise that. Why would you frame your church services to address needs you aren't aware of, or which make little impact on you and people you know?

Even the patterns for intercessions in *Common Worship* are more concerned with the powerful – rulers, royals, governors, bishops – than they are with the everyday concerns of the people in the pews. Your best chance of having your situation alluded to in most church services is to be sick or dead – experiences shared even by the ruling classes.

We badly need a change in our theology, so that it conforms more nearly with the mission of Jesus as reflected in the Gospels. When our theology is reformed, our liturgy will bring healing rather than death to the spirits of the abused. That will take a very long time and much hard work; in the meantime, we inflict further damage on those who have already suffered too much. What can we do?

Common Worship was conceived within the Church of England as a set of resources, and a framework within which to use liturgical material. Bishops seem to have rowed back somewhat on the freedom it offered; we need to reclaim it. Sometimes quite small changes can make a difference. My former colleague Stephen Callis once introduced the confession by saying, "In a time of silence, let us thank God for all the things we have got right this week." How liberating that was! Yes, we do often get things right, and we should be thankful for that.

When I was vicar of a very troubled estate, I realised how badly people needed to begin worship on a positive note. I therefore wrote a set of opening responses which began:

The night is ended
The week is over
And God is still with us
God loves us for ever.

There is an abundance of positive and affirming material we can draw on. There is enormous liturgical creativity among modern Celtic religious communities. The Iona Community and its Wee Worship Group are the most famous of these, but the Northumbria Community and the Community of Aidan and Hilda have also produced quantities of resources. Social justice, creation and nature, and the events of everyday life are common themes, so these liturgies are often helpful for survivors and other victims. The Iona Community, being earthed in a needy part of Glasgow, really excels at this.

Feminism has also been fruitful, liturgically speaking. Janet Morley and others write within an Anglican framework, so provide material which can easily be slotted into the Eucharist. A number of liturgy collections written by and for women are mindful of the experience of those who are powerless and suffering. Though they are written out of women's experience, I have found they often resonate with men as well.

The world Church, too, can come to our aid. The USPG (United Society Partners in the Gospel), Christian Aid, and the Mothers Union all publish prayers and liturgies which are gleaned from other countries and give us the benefit of their wisdom and spiritual insight. It's also worth getting prayer books from elsewhere in the Anglican Communion, where these are published in English. Usually these Churches don't have the establishment links of the C of E and therefore approach worship and the Gospel from a different angle. I have found *A New Zealand Prayer Book* and the Scottish Episcopal Church's Scottish Liturgy especially refreshing. It would be good if all English churches occasionally used such liturgies; it reminds us that we are part of a worldwide Communion, and gives other perspectives on Christianity.

In parishes which produce service sheets, it's quite easy to introduce material from the above and other sources. For the Eucharist, there is considerable freedom during the ante-communion, the intercessions, and closing responses, as long as the basic structure is followed and no heterodox doctrine is introduced. The Liturgy of the Sacrament is less flexible, but the additional material in *Common Worship* can be mined for the few gems and there are some points of flexibility. I wrote a 'Prayer of Joyful Access' to provide a positive approach to communion; a member of the committee which put together the eucharistic prayers advised me that it's 'within the spirit of' *Common Worship* and permissible to use. It has been published by the Iona Community in *Praying for the Dawn*:

Jesus, brother, you sat down at table
with women who sold their bodies,
men who sold their souls,
and those whose lives were traded by strangers.
You ate with them, and when you broke the bread
wine and laughter flowed

As we feast with you now
may your bread strengthen us,
your wine warm us,
And your love cheer us
for the days to come. Amen.

But for me, it is this prayer from Jan Berry which perhaps best sums up the 'good news' for victims:

Come to this table
where the living Christ offers us
bread broken for our journeying
and wine poured out for our tears.

Share together in this meal
where loss finds comfort in promise
and despair is transformed into hope.

Whoever you are, whatever you bring,
hear the risen Christ call your name;
and accept God's invitation to new life.

Janet Fife *was one of the first women to be ordained in the Church of England. She is a writer and survivor and has a research degree in the pastoral care of survivors. She is disabled.*

Chapter 8

Alchemy of Healing

Gilo

The courage we borrow, the courage we bring,
Shall bind us in strength to the healing we sing;
The courage to face any wound that we fear
Shall bind us in beauty and bless every tear.

Bring grace and bring kindness to all that you sing,
To heal and to honour each fierce tender thing;
Each shame left unspoken may yet shine a light;
A place that seemed broken, that place can give life.

The darkness we banish, the shadow we blame,
Though hidden, may help us to find our true name;
So bring all your courage, let all be made whole,
Transforming your story in body and soul.

Come gather your power with good friends around;
Together we stand in the truth of this ground.
Our courage can make us, can heal and can mend,
Any wound can be sacred, any wound we transcend.

Words © Gilo 2017
Tune: Columcille (Irish Melody) 11.11.11.11
www.patreon.com/Gilohymnwriter

Gilo is a survivor, hymn-writer, and outsider theologian.

Chapter 9

Paper Clip Reduction

Gilo

Is Chichester the big scandal of the Church of England? Most people assume so due to media coverage on the cover-ups in that diocese. There is an arguably greater scandal. The Past Cases Review (PCR) began in December 2007 with the Bishops' Protocol and released its result in February 2010. It lacked rigour because the hierarchy commissioning it lacked integrity and understanding. The process was seriously flawed and underestimated the scale of the problem. And those presiding over it whittled down the numbers to a ludicrously unrealistic figure.

The Church set out in its review criteria to minimise any damage which could result from opening up the books. The criteria given to reviewers were that they should include first, the number of files reviewed; second, the number referred to statutory authorities; and third, the number dealt with formally internally (Formal Church Action). There seems to have been no concern that these three criteria ignored more detailed safeguarding concerns such as cases where clergy had been arrested without being internally disciplined; retired clergy who still posed a risk; clergy against whom no action had been taken despite allegations against them; clergy with no Criminal Records Bureau (CRB) checks. Parish employees, volunteers, organists and lay readers were mostly ignored. Non-diocesan organisations such as cathedrals and monastic orders were excluded. Deceased clergy did not feature at all.

The experiences and voices of victims and survivors were entirely absent – without doubt the central failing of the PCR from the outset. Was this by design to keep a lid on the whole thing? It seems likely. One survivor offered to take part but was refused. Dioceses were instructed to keep victims at a distance from the project. It was never envisaged that this expensive paper-clip trawl might have survivors at its centre.

Amid considerable confusion, responses across dioceses varied enormously. One diocese sent a 135-page report, another a two-sentence response. One area bishop did the process himself, another bishop refused to co-operate. Some dioceses employed external reviewers as per the requirement, whilst others tasked diocesan registrars or retired clergy. And even some of the experienced professionals involved were at a loss to decipher the criteria: "I have spent the best part of two days trying to make sense of it. I have consulted two well-experienced colleagues who can't make much sense of it either," said one.

Then in 2010, after two years and £2 million on the project, the national figure of 13 cases outstanding was announced with the following declaration in an intentionally 'low-key' press release:

We firmly believe that any concerns about a member of clergy or other office holder's suitability to work with children have now been thoroughly examined in the light of current best practice by independent reviewers.

Contrast this statement with just one submission from one diocese in which 390 personnel files were reviewed and 76 were found to have had no checks at all. Of the 390 files, 24 needed further investigation. One person was ordained despite having a conviction for indecent assault. One person's file had been taken by the Metropolitan Police paedophilia squad. In another case, 'nasty' pornography was on record, but no action taken. This information does not square with the confident press release. To our knowledge, none of these cases were followed up, or investigated further at the time.

As the national results were tallied, an extraordinary process ensued in which the secretariat of the Archbishop's Council and other senior figures invited dioceses to whittle their numbers down. So, for example, in its original return, Chichester returned over 20 cases and had 60 on its known cases list. Chichester was asked to reduce the return to zero on the basis of restrictive criteria that seemed almost to have been re-invented along the way. Chichester's final return was eventually three out of the national figure of 13. Another diocese returned nearly 40 but this was reduced to zero. This seems to have been a wider pattern. We now know that Lincoln diocese has sent over 50 files to the police in recent years. Presumably some of these files might have led to action at the time of the PCR.

In short the PCR has appeared to many of us to be a national whitewash. It was never going to be anything other, we would say. It left many clergy uninvestigated, unreported to the police, and effectively protected by the Church. A mountain was shoehorned into an eggcup and those presiding over this charade hoped no one would notice the glaring misrepresentation of reality.

Sir Roger Singleton's report into the PCR came into public domain against the intended publication strategy of the Church, when details of the PCR came into the hands of the BBC. According to the BBC reporter who led the investigation, the report was still under revision two hours before it was released. Plainly the Church was 'bounced' into pre-Synod release against its wishes. The Church had hoped for a much quieter release when General Synod members had gone on holiday after the 2018 July session.

Sir Roger Singleton was critical of the Past Cases Review, its methodology and its creation of a false rosy picture with a very tiny statistic of abuse in the Church. He made the point that files were very poorly kept and called the press statement an "under-evidenced assertion". But in reality the press release he referred to looked to be a downright lie. Singleton defended the Church by denying there had been any cover-up. But his review reads like another attempt to keep things 'in house' and persuade IICSA that 'they can handle it'. Through emollient terms he failed to call the PCR what many of us believe it was – organised massage of the figures which hid abuse and allowed perpetrators and the good name of the Church to be protected.

He missed a key point, which is that the PCR was largely a statistical exercise unconcerned with rigorous assessment of Church responses. There was no assessment of whether the Church response in each case was appropriate (i.e. whether the alleged perpetrator had been treated too leniently or whether a case was reported to the police). He also failed to recognise that cover-up can be nuanced. The PCR didn't need active cover-up, didn't require anyone to say out loud, "let's hide these things". This is because so much passive cover-up was already in place. Through the various layers of personnel involved, all that was required was subtle pressure to follow the path of least resistance despite the confusion of highly restrictive criteria. No objections were raised. This passivity is summed up neatly by former Safeguarding Advisor, Pearl Luxon, in her evidence to IICSA:

> My recollection is that the bishops and the C of E as a whole were averse to exposing themselves to any greater scrutiny than was strictly necessary. The plea for transparency and openness, which Bishop Anthony Priddis put to them at the outset of the proposal, was limited over time and in outcome.

Had the Archbishops Council thrown bingo numbers in the air and grabbed one at random, the result would have been more accurate. Any number higher than13! The final weeks leading up to the press release, which became the overriding focus, degenerated into surreal farce. Senior figures presiding over the debacle messaged each other back and forth with yet more whittling down of numbers. Their confusion, by this stage quite conscious, lasted right up to the week before the 2010 press release. These were people at the top of the chain who had governed the whole process. The simplest description I've heard of this process by one of the IICSA lawyers: "it was seedy".

They were still at this late stage working out how many Formal Church Actions to include and seemed to even wonder whether further reductions they were carrying out might raise questions about the integrity of the process. Their own discomfort at the inconsistency seems to comes across loud and clear. It would also appear that a clear message was given that any return to dioceses to check on cases was out of the question.

It is not difficult to see an underlying focus on self-protection from public ridicule. Remarkably, not one bishop recognised that they had commissioned what was in effect a national whitewash. If any did recognise this, it went unvoiced. Perhaps not surprising. A few months prior to the PCR Bishops' Protocol in 2007, the bishops had privately agreed to an instruction from the Church's senior legal officer to take part in "careful drafting" of semblanced apologies to avoid concession of legal liability. Hoodwink apologies in complicity with their insurers, as others of us would see it. So it is perhaps no surprise that the PCR turned out as it did – an avoidance of responsibility on an industrial scale.

Were there intakes of breath around dioceses when the tally of 13 cases requiring action was issued? MACSAS (Minister and Clergy Sexual Abuse Survivors) alerted the Church to the craziness of the thing by asking if this included 22 and rising that they were aware of in one diocese alone. The question was ignored. No bishop made any public utterance on the absurdity of it all across the past eight years. At least 15 current bishops were involved in the PCR at that time.

In 2015 the UK Methodist Church produced the results of its Past Cases Review. The figure was nearly 2,000 cases. The Methodist Church is about a quarter of the size of the Church of England. And these will be the recorded cases on file. There will be many unrecorded cases too. C of E strategy is laid bare when put alongside Methodist willingness to be transparent and really open their books to daylight.

All of this shows the necessity for removal of the Church's safeguarding and response to survivors from its control. The Church cannot be trusted to mark its own homework. Despite statements to the contrary, it is still not being transparent. In 2013 Archbishop Sentamu made a public show of ordering a review of all deceased clergy files in York diocese: a good and necessary decision and one we believe other dioceses have copied. But no one knows the result, as it was never made public. Why trumpet a review but then hide the figures? Each statistic represents a passage of harm and neglect. This invisibility displays a powerfully inbuilt reluctance to invite survivors forward. Victims and survivors have had little presence. Elizabeth Hall, a former national advisor to the Church, highlighted the particular dysfunctionality of York diocese in her IICSA statement when she compared the effectiveness of the Archbishops' provincial palaces:

> At Bishopthorpe, which is much smaller than Lambeth, this expertise and resource time was simply not available. For example, the Archbishop of York's chaplain received most of the initial safeguarding contacts (typically adults reporting church-based abuse), and it seemed to be only when she was convinced about the matter that it even went any further within the Church, let alone to the police.

How can there be confidence in such a structure? One of the uncomfortable tasks of General Synod is to hold the senior layer to much greater account, rather than blindly accepting the serving up of smoke and mirrors. Members need comprehensive information, facts and figures, background papers and preparatory debate to make sense of the history leading to any of the leadership's current prescribed proposals. They also need to be able to frame questions without the obstruction and stymieing that some Synod members have told us occurs. The questions need to include explanatory context for the benefit of those in Synod who do not follow these matters so closely. By giving so little opportunity for real debate and almost no briefing material, the senior ranks of the Church of England seem to treat their General Synod with disdain and maintain docility. They keep them in the semi-dark. So far the list of crucial things gone undebated by Synod include the Kendall House Review, Elliott Review, Gibb Report, PCR, 2 Carlile Reports, IICSA pt 1. The present structures do not facilitate engagement or an effective informed critique, and is protective of the status quo

Incidentally the last two times survivors have sat in Synod's public gallery, we have been struck by the presence of three senior figures in denial on the raised platform. How can there be movement forward whilst bishops who have driven far up cul-de-sacs of denial continue to be protected by a docile deference? The hierarchy quietly shields itself, and no one in a senior position challenges their peers towards honesty. And so the culture that informed the PCR is present still – one of denial and fear coupled with an intent to hide things.

Had the Church been transparent, the Known Cases Lists (some of which have vanished in the past decade) drawn up in each diocese would have given a much more accurate presentation of abuse hidden across time. Not the whole picture, as many cases went unrecorded – but it would at least have shown that the Church was aware by 2010 of a very significant problem. It is this failing, born out of a wilful decision to only reveal what was deemed strictly necessary, which senior figures have been scared of confronting and owning across the last decade. We have not yet heard any senior figure speak authentically about the industrial-scale whitewash that took place. Nor has anyone been held to any kind of account.

A Parable

Jesus asked his followers to gather up all those harmed by the Church.

Any survivors of abuse. So he might heal and transform their lives with justice and compassion.

His followers spent many pieces of silver on a hunt. They shifted and shunted stories around with much confusion and chaos. Many stories of harm were overlooked and excluded. Many hundreds were briefly looked at, only to be cast aside.

Eventually they came to Jesus and drew him away from the crowd.

"We have found thirteen" they whispered, and put thirteen paper-clips into his outstretched hand. They hoped he would not notice the deception.

Jesus wept. And turned towards Golgotha.

Gilo is a survivor, hymn-writer, and outsider theologian.

Chapter 10

The Church that Buckles at the Knee?

Gilo

A letter sent to all Church of England bishops in the summer of 2016.

I call on the House of Bishops to repent at your meeting in York at the end of this week. Others in the survivor community are saying the same. Repentance implies action and not just words – it is about turning around 180 degrees and starting again. The crisis this senior layer has brought upon itself has finally woken the church up to the need for real change. If the bishops hope to delay changes as we are told you might, the situation will be acutely embarrassing. It is a worrying indication of a culture in denial and paralysis that no bishop has commented on the Elliott Report since it came out in mid March – 100% silence. Perhaps your strategists have given instructions to ignore it and ride the storm out. I think their advice present in much of your hidden structure of response to survivors has been spectacularly bad. It has led you away from the values of your own gospel and narrative.

I am urging Bishop Paul Butler, Bishop Tim Thornton and Archbishop Justin Welby to lead a call for repentance across the whole House of Bishops. All these bishops have involvement in my case. Denial of disclosures to senior figures ("no recollection") and blanking of crucial questions by the bishop I reported to were main features of the church's response in the findings of that report. Along with reckless compliance to the demands of Ecclesiastical, your own insurer. And silence from Lambeth Palace to more than a dozen cries for help. Similar experiences of many other survivors from what MACSAS (Ministers and Clergy Sexual Abuse Survivors) tell me – indicate many other bishops know the same powerful criticisms apply to them. This cuts across the board.

The House of Bishops needs to show clearly that you are finally able beyond the eleventh hour to work rapidly for profound change in your culture and structure – arising from honest acceptance of the mess you have made. Survivors will know the weight is lifted when we see the Church willing to buckle beneath the weight of the questions and all the impact – that we carry on the Church's behalf. When we see the Church being honest and transparent in its answers to questions – then we'll know the weight is shifting to where it belongs. The senior layer needs to dig its way out of the hole you have dug yourselves into. Cover-ups, denials, obscuring of issues, intentional inertia, fog, smoke and mirrors, blanking of questions, unchallenged power of bishops, legal games, incestuous dependence on your own insurer to limit liability, unethical closing down of cases, withdrawal of support on the instructions of EIG, bewilderingly adversarial settlements – all of which I and many others have experienced – all this must come to an end in real repentance. So that survivors, those of us currently on the way through a process and many others yet to come forward, are responded to safely and sanely. You can no longer operate a mirage in which Responding Well (the Church's published policy set on response to survivors) can be torn in two to suit the interests of your own insurer – especially when the aims and actions of EIG run so malevolently counter to your own stated guidelines. This mirage is rotten, can only do further harm, and must now stop. You need to disentangle your response to this problem from your own insurer – it has led you into deep complicity and does enormous damage to both survivors and yourselves.

But you know what to do. You have been told many times through regular visits of survivors to Lambeth Palace and repeated challenges to your Head of Safeguarding. Challenges to so many of you in fact – from survivors and others, both in person and through growing number of articles in the press. You cannot wait for more waves of crisis to hit you before finally doing the right thing. If you continue to rely on the tenacity of survivors to do all the painful work of trying to transform your structure – the IICSA Inquiry will be over and the Church you lead will look powerfully diminished. Senior leaders and bishops need to show tenacity yourselves and act quickly now to transform the situation for everyone. This starts with repentance and real action arising from a commitment to change. If you can make this collective decision at this critical House of Bishops assembly – you are likely to move forward through the Inquiry and everything yet to emerge with greater grace and much less pain. And better prospect of healing for everyone, including yourselves. The Church can hold its head high knowing it is doing the right thing. If you make the wrong decisions – well, it seems obvious to survivors that there is no grass left to kick changes into. The crisis will be acute and can only deepen. The Elliott

Report into my case could be repeated across so many survivor experiences – as similar issues have appeared again and again elsewhere. I don't know how much more embarrassing you need a Report to be, so it astonishes me and other survivors I am in contact with – to hear that the House of Bishops might try and delay changes. I urge you not to. I urge you to repent.

A speech delivered to a General Synod Fringe Meeting in July 2018

This speech was made on the eve of the Safeguarding debate. It was addressed directly and calmly to both Archbishops and others, including about 50 Synod members.

Archbishop Justin, I've got to know several John Smyth victims. There are now about 90 victims in the UK and Africa, which makes Smyth possibly the Jimmy Savile of the C of E. Or one of them. I met one survivor a week ago when he came to visit me and we had lunch on the beach near where I live. And several of the Smyth victims have asked me to say this to you, Archbishop.

They still have not had an answer as to why you sat on the 2013 disclosure for four years, and as far as they are aware, did nothing? And why, after a year and half, they have been continually told they will not be allowed to meet you. These were your friends, fellow Iwerne Officers and campers. You said on LBC early last year "they've been grievously and deeply let down". They still feel that. You were mentor to the man I had fish and chips with last week. These were your people.

This crisis of the senior layer isn't going away. Not until it's faced properly and honestly. The crisis of leadership runs across the senior layer. It includes you, Archbishop Justin. But it also includes you, Archbishop Sentamu, and two other senior bishops, in current police investigation. One of these bishops sits on the National Safeguarding Steering Group alongside another bishop in denial. MACSAS is aware that nearly a third of current diocesan bishops have responded to survivors dishonourably. This deepening crisis cannot be managed away or hidden. It is a crisis that can only change by being transformed. Your communications teams, advisors, reputation managers, and all that I call the strategariat – they can't do this. They're not trained to transform. They're trained to hide, protect, shield, to Teflon coat, present truth in a cloak.

What happens when this crisis and all this denial trickles down into the kingdoms of deference beneath bishop-level into diocesan structures or into a dysfunctional National Safeguarding Team in Church

House? At best the crisis creates a culture of cognitive dissonance. The denial spreads. At worst it can turn into real delinquency. In one diocese a member of the Safeguarding Advisory Committee said to me down the phone, "What did you expect me to do – go bang on the door of Lambeth Palace for you?" in a mocking sarcastic tone, before putting the phone down. I don't understand how this theology belongs in any diocese, let alone a Safeguarding Advisory Committee! That was said after I'd written 17 letters to Lambeth Palace. This is an ugly theology.

I think there's only one person that can transform all this. And that's you, Archbishop. No one in the rest of your structure can or will. Bishop Peter Hancock can't. Bishop Sarah Mullally can't. Nobody can. Except you. And it will either be you … or the next archbishop who finally finds the courage and sense of leadership to transform all this. My feeling is that instead of acting like a prisoner trapped inside your own broken structure, you should get on with it? I suspect that will start with honesty about Iwerne, and a willingness to meet your old friends. They were your people.

If you don't transform this, you and other bishops will continue to dash your own Church on the rocks of your own moral and theological crisis.

£200 million is missing?

In the second mediation Bishop Paul Butler tabled £200 million as a potential redress fund to help people back on their feet. That's missing from tomorrow's Synod debate. It's vanished. The bishops don't recognise life-long impact from abuse. Nor do you recognise the impact for many of us of reporting to a rotten structure. Life for many has not got better – it has got worse or much more complicated. If I could turn the clock back I would! But this is common. Survivors are routinely harmed and re-abused by this structure.

Phil Johnson says every meeting he attends at Church House or Lambeth Palace, everyone around the table is on salaried time – except survivors! Survivors do all the driving of change – and then eventually you react when you can no longer hide from or absorb the embarrassment – but you don't honour the work or time or expertise of survivors at all. The structure washes its hands of the cost to us of the massive task of taking on your structure. And I wonder when was the last time any bishop contacted the many people who've limped away jaded, angry and embittered at having to deal with such a dysfunctional and often malevolent structure. When are you going to take that seriously?

Not tomorrow – that's for sure.

Until you put survivors back on our feet properly with compassionate justice and a willingness to put real money to helping lift people up – tomorrow's debate is just a mirage. April Alexander (Church Commissioner and respected synod member) said it better than I can.

Reasonable and pastoral settlement criteria would do no more than help survivors pick up their lives again and to live decently while they do so. Without reasonable financial settlements there is little the Church or anyone else can do to enable survivors to pick up their lives at all.

If she can get it – and many others in Synod too – why can't the bishops?

Gilo is a survivor, hymn-writer, and outsider theologian.

Chapter 11

The Virtuous Circle

Gilo

This chapter explores the deep-rooted affiliation between the Church of England and its insurer Ecclesiastical Insurance. First some background history. Ecclesiastical Fire Insurance was created in 1887 by C of E members to provide for the Church's own insurance needs, perceived at that time in terms of fire risk alone. Self-insurance was common among religious institutions. The Methodists were first, creating their insurance company 15 years earlier. It made economic sense – money went out from individual churches and returned to central coffers to support the work of the Church.

For nearly a century Ecclesiastical was effectively owned by the C of E. Then in 1972 the Church created Allchurches Trust Ltd to take on legal ownership of the insurer. The signatories of incorporation included both Archbishops at the time, Michael Ramsey and Donald Coggan, plus the Dean of St Paul's, Archdeacon of Lincoln, and Secretary General of Synod and other C of E figures. All were acting as senior officers of the Church, and ATL was perceived as a C of E body.

In the decades that followed, Ecclesiastical gradually acquired other companies to become Ecclesiastical Insurance Group (EIG). They own Ansvar, one of the main insurers of UK charities, and Lycetts, a major equine and farm/estate insurance provider, amongst others. The group involves several layers of ownership with some subsidiary companies owning smaller subsidiaries. But the whole group is owned by Allchurches Trust Ltd (ATL), and run as a charitable enterprise. Profit from EIG goes to ATL which distributes grants to churches and charities around the UK and elsewhere.

In 1987 EIG created an investment management house to provide savings and investment products for clergy and dioceses. Originally called Ecclesiastical Investment, it was rebranded in 2015 to EdenTree as 'Ecclesiastical' was considered off-putting for an investment house seeking to widen its client base beyond clergy. EdenTree is also fully owned by ATL and gives profit to the mother-lode.

In 2016 EIG and the Church of England celebrated £50 million of donations to ATL within 3 years, with a special service in Gloucester Cathedral at which a letter of thanks from Archbishop Welby was read out. It demonstrated without any doubt the close affiliation of the insurer to the Church of England. Emphasis was given to the many small charities that EIG supports, and the whole enterprise seems on the surface the 'virtuous circle' that Sir Philip Mawer (ATL Chair) describes in a short promotional film of the event.

Many small charities do indeed benefit from this business. But what EIG and its owner ATL are perhaps less keen to give prominence to, is the funding priority to C of E Dioceses through 'block grants'. Their annual reports and Companies House filing history give a stark picture. ATL gives between 80 per cent and 90 per cent annually to the C of E and to Anglican churches. In 2014 the total shared between C of E dioceses, cathedrals, and churches was 92 per cent of that year's grants. This is a major cash cow for the Church of England.

Senior Clerics on EIG board of directors

The Church, EIG and ATL have all claimed "the Church is simply another client" and that the insurer is entirely separate from the Church. Whilst this may be legally accurate, Companies House records show high-ranking clerics on the board of directors of EIG across the past four decades. Archdeacons, deans and bishops have been involved in running the insurer. Sir Philip Mawer, former Secretary General of the C of E Synod, has been on the board twice; the first time during his years serving as the Church's most senior civil servant. Currently there is only one senior cleric on the board. It may be coincidental, but during decades of cover-up, the board had three or four senior Church figures at a time. For example in 1993 there were an archdeacon, two cathedral deans and a bishop – over a third of the board. That's considerable institutional heft and influence. It's not hard to imagine the embedded deference, spheres of loyalty, patronage, and mutual interest that have accompanied so much hierarchy. A bishop in any boardroom is likely to receive the deference in the room. A board with three or four senior clerics cannot in any way be characterized as a "Church is simply another client" situation – as all parties in this nexus have tried to claim. The Church needs to be a good deal more honest about this corporate affiliation and the flow of money.

This powerful nexus throws up many ethical questions. I tried to engage both Church and insurer with these conflict-of-interest questions for nearly two years. There was no will to address them. A member of the National Safeguarding Team treated the questions with hostility and outright boredom during a malevolent meeting in Church House. When raised with the National Advisor and Lead Bishop, the questions drew a blank. When raised with two trustees of ATL in the presence of Ian Elliott just after the Elliott Review, an irritated retort from one senior cleric was, "We don't own our own insurer". This senior cleric sat on the board of Trustees that owns the insurer, and also on the Archbishops' Independent Safeguarding Panel at the time. If that's not a conflict of interest, I'm not sure what is? It's not surprising that many survivors feel the Church's National Safeguarding is in place to safeguard institution, hierarchy and insurer.

Most people don't need a degree in 'corporate' to recognise moral affiliation and the moral responsibility that should accompany it. The two may be legally separate. But in terms that most people would understand, the two are morally and institutionally joined at the hip. These two corporate cultures have clearly shaped and reinforced each other over the decades. EIG regularly attended the Church's central safeguarding committee from the mid 1990s right through to 2015. It's a strange picture when accompanying the silencing and cover-ups so many survivors have experienced. Would it be likely that senior Church figures in Ecclesiastical have been club-able with other bishops who've covered up abuse in the past? We have seen from the letters of influence in one case the mention of Nobody's Friends, a secretive Lambeth Palace dining club. And in another case two members of the Nikaean Club, another Lambeth Palace dining club, rallied to the aid of a former club chairman at his trial. One of those who helped was a former archbishop and the other later became a bishop.

If any of the bishops on the board of EIG directors were approached by survivors in their dioceses – would they, as part of their pastoral response, have informed them of the potential conflict of interest? Have these senior clerics been advised to encourage other bishops to turn a blind eye? And ultimately, to whom have these hierarchs owed allegiance? The Church and its stated pastoral aims, or does fiduciary responsibility to the insurer claim priority? These are just some of the questions raised by this interwoven nexus. But cognitive dissonance and denial in C of E culture seems to prevent senior figures, or a too deferential Safeguarding, from engaging with them.

The image is of a church that pretends a 'robust' response whilst consciously operating a mirage. In a whistle-blown House of Bishops document published in 2015, the C of E's legal head advised diocesan bishops to use "careful drafting" to

"effectively apologise" without enabling victims to get compensation. The Church and insurer have in effect both been washing their hands of responsibility for actions of the other, whilst maintaining the pretence of separation.

Because of the possibility that statements of regret might have the unintended effect of accepting legal liability for the abuse it is important that they are approved in advance by lawyers, as well as by diocesan communications officers (and, if relevant, insurers). With careful drafting it should be possible to express them in terms which effectively apologise for what has happened whilst at the same time avoiding any concession of legal liability for it.

No bishop commented on the House of Bishops document when it emerged. A nameless spokesperson issued a three line defence. This corporate strategy of the 'creature from the crypt' serves to bat all questions away. No one can ask a spokesperson any further question. They retreat back into the shadows as fast as they emerged – a good way of killing a story. Yet the policy and culture hidden in that document since 2007 involved all of the senior layer, and ran totally counter to the Church's stated aims in Responding Well. This was a moment when bishops might have taken ownership of the deceptive mirage played out on survivors.

Instead the article met a wall of silence as bishops ran to ground. Survivors are familiar with this deafening roar of omertà from a Church which only seems to respond when embarrassment is sufficiently acute. One wonders whether any bishop stood up at the time, when the advice was issued by their senior lawyer, to say "It's not my role to be an adjunct to an insurer – my role is to be a pastor and heal survivors, not hoodwink them." Perhaps some did say something like this privately. But they didn't have enough moxie to speak out.

Minister and Clergy Sexual Abuse Survivors (MACSAS) know that many survivors could match this document to their own experience of the Church's response. It certainly echoed the blanking and silencing of major questions by senior bishops leading up to the Elliott Review. Ultimately 17 letters to Archbishop Welby were ignored, apparently on the advice of the insurers and lawyers acting on their behalf. Finally after colossal effort, two bishops – the Bishop of Durham and the former Bishop of Truro – came to mediation to account for the blanking of these questions and give personal apology. To my mind it is the insurers who helped dig these bishops into such an uncomfortable and embarrassing position. That and a culture of denial and fear in the senior layer. And poor theology.

Perhaps after sufficient change of culture and structure, and fear of honesty no longer holds bishops in thrall – then mediation might be a way forward. Eventually the Church will put its hands up and start being transparent. In the two mediations I took part in with two bishops, one bishop was genuinely contrite and clearly keen that the Church moved forward. But given how easy it is for the Church to deploy smoke and mirrors, I now believe the only way forward will be a Truth and Reconciliation council involving as many as want to take part.

Virtuous Circle?

The Church of England is making exponentially rising amounts of money from a major insurance business. Some dioceses encourage parishes to regard Ecclesiastical as the 'official insurer' of the diocese and in effect the only go-to. There are currently only two insurance companies for C of E churches to choose from, Ecclesiastical and Trinitas, but Ecclesiastical insures the vast majority – about 95 per cent. This effective monopoly clearly benefits dioceses, one of the major beneficiaries of the charitable enterprise. It's entirely up to the Church of England how it wants to manage part of its corporate affairs. But if that involves a contaminated structure in which survivors are being further harmed – then it needs bringing into daylight.

Indeed, many C of E survivors have been harmed by the Church's hand-wash and

toxic fusion of pastoral and legal games. The C of E needs to sort out its broken culture and acknowledge the embedded conflict of interest and corruption in this nexus. They need to recognise the need for urgent structural change. The 'circle' will only recover virtue in the eyes of survivors when the Church creates an authentic redress system – one that is fair, dignified, transparent, and focused on healing and mending of lives – to replace the adversarial roller-coaster of 'horse trade' games the C of E relies upon the insurer to play out on its behalf. If the Church wanted, it could almost overnight begin to remove the toxic barriers (blanking, silencing, amnesia, denial, legal games, closing down of cases, fog and obfuscation, complicity, hand-washing...) that cause much additional suffering to survivors.

I am not the first to raise these questions. Bishop Paul Butler and Archbishop Welby buried their heads in the sand for five years, to repeated challenges from MACSAS about 'smoke and mirrors'. The

Church needs to give shape to a transparent response to survivors that helps put people back on their feet in real ways. Compensation and redress for harm should be the beginning of a pastoral relationship with a healing community – and not the last word, a box-tick, followed by ecclesial hand-wash.

Legal Games?

Let's drill down a little into how EIG operates. I'll use my own case as an example. The Bishop of Durham explained, in a Clergy CDM response and in the mediations, that the EIG solicitor had approached him with a list of possible legal defences that might be used against me. The bishop to his credit said that he did not want these used, as he recognised that the defences proposed were ugly and would not reflect particularly well on the Church – and anyway, the Church had accepted my case fully. The EIG lawyer apparently agreed to follow his wishes, but then behind his back went on to use every single one of those defences in a profoundly distressing horse-trade. The Bishop of Durham later told us he was appalled and dismayed when he found out. But then, to add insult to injury – EIG argued publicly that they had not taken part in the Elliott Review and therefore had no opportunity to state their position. This is simply not the case. The lawyer representing EIG and who had led the settlement was present at two core groups run by the National Advisor, to which my solicitor and myself were not invited. We were not even informed. So the EIG representative had a ringside seat at core groups discussing 'pastoral' response – and was able in effect to cover her tracks from an adversarial settlement which had taken place only weeks before. This lawyer met Ian Elliott twice, and after one of those core groups was invited to state the insurer's policies at the time. Ecclesiastical had ample opportunity to represent themselves in that Review – but at the time had zero policies towards care for survivors in their settlement procedure. I am not entirely sure the policies they have now have made much difference.

EIG appears to many people concerned with these issues to speak with a forked tongue, but are protected from tough questions and answers by the shield of Church House. It's a powerful nexus and one in which honesty looks to be a shifting commodity. Ian Elliott and myself tried, he for two years, to get Church House to address highly misleading public statements made by EIG. But eventually we had to give up. We recognised that the insurer's hold over Church House officials was simply too strong. They are presumably in thrall to this nexus and cannot say the right or honest thing – because to do so would compromise the relationship in which the Church makes many millions each year.

The fusion of the pastoral and the legal is extraordinary, and has probably contaminated most abuse cases the Church has responded to. It has suited the insurer to see the Church blanking, fogging, denying and avoiding crucial questions – and in my opinion there is evidence to suggest that the insurer has actively encouraged or even instructed the Church to do so. In my own case, the Bishop of Durham clearly told the Elliott Review that he was instructed by the insurer to withdraw all pastoral support and end contact. So too the London Diocesan Safeguarding Adviser at the time. In my view, though they may deny it, EIG have plenty of form in this. They share in considerable corporate power in tandem with the Church, but the corporate veil has been raised and torn in two.

As has the temple veil of the Church.

Gilo is a survivor, hymn-writer, and outsider theologian.

Chapter 12

Last Man Standing

Graham

How far are you prepared to go?

I am a Smyth victim. John Smyth QC viciously beat about 30 schoolboys and undergraduates. His diabolical regime lasted about four years and is well documented elsewhere as a matter of public record. In a 1982 report for the Iwerne Trust, Canon Mark Ruston estimated that Smyth inflicted an estimated 14,000 strokes of the cane, which created wounds that bled profusely and had to be bandaged. I will not dwell on that. My memory has compartmentalised that somewhere I cannot retrieve it, for now.

What I do have, though I cannot remember it from then, is a chilling, chilling reminder of the grooming and persuasion. I cannot explain why we succumbed, why intelligent Oxbridge undergraduates would ever consent to what was inflicted upon us. However, I have a text, twisted by that mad man's logic, that raises the hairs on the back of my neck. My copy of *The Making of a Man of God,* by Alan Redpath, is inscribed with my name and "20.X.81, Chapter 26" in the handwriting of John Smyth.

In 1981, the book was used to persuade me of the scriptural basis for the beatings; of my need for them, and my need to prove my devotion and commitment. In hindsight that meant my commitment to the elite that Iwerne represented, and my commitment to the chosen few that Smyth had around him. I underlined passages of it, presumably with Smyth, on 20 October 1981. I cannot remember doing so, but they bring a chill, a shudder that now frightens me. Others can recall biblical "justification" for Smyth's proposals. I cannot.

I am actually not going to comment further. I am just going to list much of what I underlined back then.

> To educate and refine the flesh so that it becomes profitable in His service is never God's plan. He insists on the sentence of death upon everything that you and I are in ourselves ... There is only one place for all that is "self" – on Calvary. (page 13)

> What many of us today need is a burning examination by the Holy Spirit, which may be bitter to the taste but which may awaken us to the disaster of us imagining that we are Christians when there is no evidence in our lives of His Grace. (page 16)

Then Chapter 26.

> He has planned for you a personal Calvary, a personal Pentecost, and where His blessings must be withheld until, like David, you prostrate yourself in sackcloth on your face before Him ... Observe then the price that David paid. The experience of humiliation was to be followed by one of worship ... But David's answer was a firm No: "I will verily buy it for the full price. For I will not take that which is thine for the Lord ... without cost." (page 243).

> Tell me, have you been up Mt Moriah? I trust you have been up Mt Calvary and therefore have received forgiveness and cleansing by the blood that was shed for you ... There is always one point in each life where the spiritual battle is crucial. Have you faced it? Have you gone up to Mt Moriah? Have you paid the price? Or has Satan made you feel content that you have dealt with other things, that you have given up much in your life, although you hold tenaciously to that which you now know mars your testimony... (page 244)

> That is all he wants of us, because from that platform where the self life has been truly crushed and reduced to ashes, the Lord can then display in all His glory. (page 245)

The pages quoted are from my 1980 reprint of the 1962 original.

Last Man Standing

In 2012 I disclosed historical abuse by John Smyth to the Church of England. Six years later, I am worn out. From my point of view the following pertains – there has been no meaningful response from the C of E; the Titus Trust, where John Smyth was chairman, has refused to engage at all, and has never taken responsibility; I have no idea where the police investigation has reached. The National Safeguarding Team (NST) has shown not the slightest interest; and I have been told that I cannot have contact with the Core Group as "the Core Group is set up in relation to the perpetrator, not the victim(s), with a focus on safeguarding". I have had 18 months of counselling from a psychologist, but that has had to be paid for privately.

So, do I just give up ? Do I walk away, defeated? Have the combined inactions of all concerned been effective? They have just ground me down so that I have no option, for my health, but to walk away.

But I am still angry. And my anger is aimed at Archbishop Justin Welby. At the Independent Inquiry into Child Sexual Abuse (IICSA) Archbishop Welby made a very strong statement: "Nobody can say 'it's not my fault ... it was someone else's job to report it.' That is not an acceptable human response, yet alone a leadership response. If you know a child is being abused, not to report it is simply wrong." He had said just before that, "It is quite clear that if people don't report it, it is a disciplinary matter."

In 2012 I disclosed John Smyth's abuse. This was, by Justin Welby's own admission, brought to his attention in 2013. However, he then did nothing with the allegations. This is despite the fact that he worked with John Smyth at the Iwerne camps; he exchanged Christmas cards with Smyth, who visited him in Paris; and he described Smyth as "charming and delightful". This is very close to Welby, and surely alarm bells rang ? But, he failed to follow up, and assumed that the Bishop of Ely was dealing with it. Is this not exactly the disciplinary offence that Welby describes above? In fact, the Diocese of Ely write to Smyth's present Diocese of Cape Town, but did not hear back. An Ely DSA (Diocesan Safeguarding Adviser) wrote to me in 2014:

> Unfortunately I have no power to compel agencies in South Africa to respond to my concerns and no professional routes to take this further. I know this will be difficult for you to hear and I am sorry that I am unable to say something more positive.

After the Channel 4 documentary exposing Smyth, allegations continued to emerge from South Africa about Smyth's continuing inappropriate contact with adolescents and young men up until 2016. Did the inactivity of Justin Welby mean Smyth's abuse continued after 2012–13? On Christmas Day 2013, a Smyth victim attempted suicide: this was *after* Welby knew about it and this should never, ever have happened.

When Archbishop Welby was interviewed by Nick Ferrari on LBC radio a few days after the story broke, I found myself shouting at the screen. Welby referred to a "rigorous enquiry". I was the only victim to have come forward then, and never met or was interviewed by anyone from the Diocese of Ely, Lambeth, the police, or Safeguarding. There was no rigorous enquiry. Welby then stated that, "I went to live in Paris in '78 and came back in '83 and had no contact with the camps at all." He clearly tried to distance himself from Iwerne camps. However, he was subsequently shown to have visited the camps in that period. His biography states (page 35) that, "Welby was involved in the camps as an undergraduate and again as a businessman and theological college student in the 1980s and early 1990s"(page 35). From my perspective, he gave a very misleading impression during that radio interview.

Archbishop Welby was also asked by Nick Ferrari, "What's your message to the victims?" He replied, "My message is very simple: that that should never have happened, that their interests have to come first. That those are the people we care about most ... They really, really matter." He went on to say, "Nobody has any chance of covering up, all that is in place now, and all that is essential because we want to put survivors first."

These feel hollow words to me, and they make me so angry. The Smyth victim group has still had no direct contact, that I am aware of, with Archbishop Justin Welby. There has been no taking responsibility by anyone. He "meets with victims" regularly, we are told, though not with his old friends; his co-officers at Iwerne, his public school and Cambridge friends', his "tribe."

Last Man Standing. Since the Smyth abuse was disclosed in 2012, I am aware of the following among the victim group among the victim group: one suicide attempt; one person Sectioned; at least five people needing professional psychiatric help. At IICSA, Archbishop Welby said,

> What is clear to me is that, at the moment, everything seems to take a very, very long time ... It can take three or four years, and you end up damaging the victims and survivors more. You abuse them in the way you keep them waiting.

That damage has been done.

I find myself alone now. The other victims I have been talking to are exhausted, unwell, and have been advised to withdraw from the battle for justice. We have tried to engage with the NST and the Core Group (whoever they are; we are not allowed to know). We have written endlessly, just to try to get a response. We have goaded, stirred. Anything to get a response.

But victims do not come first. Archbishop Welby does not appear to us to "care about [them] most". Our interests do not "come first". Every attempt has been made to cover up the failures in 2013, which were "not an acceptable human response, yet alone a leadership response" according to his own words.

So, I give up. I am exhausted. You win.

'Graham' is a survivor of the Iwerne camps and John Smyth.

Chapter 13

An Entirely Different Approach: The Church of England and Survivors of Abuse

Andrew Graystone

In a May 2019 email to senior church leaders I pleaded for "an entirely different approach" in the Church's relationship with victims of abuse in church contexts. Bishop Sarah Mullally encouraged me to spell out what that might look like. This is my brief attempt to explain.

The nature of abuse is to inflict trauma on the personhood of the victim. It is a conscious invasion, intended to violently challenge and destabilise the physical, sexual, cultural and/or spiritual identity of the Other – to fundamentally devalue their Otherness and forcefully mark them with the identity of the abuser. In other words, abuse is intrinsically relational. Where the abuser is ontologically identified with an organisation or culture, as in the case of teacher, sports coach or church officer for example, the identity that is marked includes that of the organisation.

So a victim abused by a clergyman is indelibly marked as a victim of church abuse, and the relationship that is damaged is not only that between the victim and their abuser, but also between the victim and the institution. Victims of abuse in church contexts are baptised, not into the identity of Christ, but into a false baptism as a worthless object for the pleasure of the church. Many church leaders fail to understand this, and act as if, in their dealings with victims, they are simply being asked to make good the acts of a previous generation, for which they feel somewhat grudgingly responsible. In fact the role of church leaders is to robustly reverse the previous messages, and affirm the worth and identity of the broken victim as a true icon of Christ.

Because the nature of abuse is ontological, healing from abuse is categorically different from other kinds of reparation. A victim of fraud may be compensated with money, such that reparation reaches a point of full repayment. If there is a dispute about damages, it may be resolved by mediation. A victim of accidental injury may be physically treated so that their wounds reach a point of complete healing.

A person whose human identity has been radically traumatised by abuse will never achieve completion, but may have a lifelong struggle with issues of identity and value. Many church leaders understand this from their own experience, but Anglican ecclesiology and culture leaves very little room for leaders to acknowledge their own vulnerability in this area. As a result, most of those who carry the wounds of abuse themselves choose not to speak about them, or if they do, to insist that they have had no lasting effects.

Ironically, those survivors who say that they are content with the way that the church has treated them may be unwittingly saying that they are able to internalise the devalued identity that has been given to them, whilst those survivors who continue to protest are saying to the church, "I am still here, and I still matter." The latter group has the most to teach a church that is, if truth were told, struggling with its own identity and victimhood in a society where it is increasingly Othered by the culture.

Sadly, instead of seeing the theological and missional opportunity presented by the current crisis of abuse, the church currently chooses to relate to survivors through the managerial culture of the secular polity. Allegations of abuse are seen as legacy problems in the smooth running of the institution. Abuse is constructed as an event requiring an economic and managerial solution, rather than a ruptured relationship requiring restoration. Instead of embracing victims as wounded strangers on the Jericho road, bishops greet each fresh revelation as a problem. That is why the church's response over the last ten years has been to produce policy, mandate training, increase budgets, and refer to lawyers and insurers – and where possible to avoid or minimise responsibility.

Of course, the impact of this on a victim, who is continuing to come to terms with their ruptured personhood, is to see the church once again trying to impose its own identity, and to minimise the value of the broken individual in relation to the powerful institution. This is what victims sometimes describe as "re-abuse" – the contemporary church adding its endorsement to the messages of the original abuser.

Very often a victim approaches the church thinking, "Perhaps disclosing my abuse could be a step towards rebuilding my identity?" In practice they find themselves face to face with a bishop thinking, "How can I fix this new problem, whilst minimising the cost and reputational damage to the church?" Victims of abuse are often deeply shocked to discover that the church is going to adopt such an adversarial approach to them.

But a radically alternative approach *is* possible. For Christians, the resurrection of Christ represents a comprehensive and definitive disruption of the natural order. The message of the resurrection is not merely that what has been broken can be restored – though it is that. Nor is it simply that the church can weather the greatest of disasters. Resurrection ruptures the meaning and order of the universe, making non-sense of our ordered managerialism, and fundamentally undermining the church's self-perception. In the resurrection the church acknowledges that it cannot make sense of itself, and into this chaos, God breathes life.

The church that fails to embrace the disorder of the resurrection cannot experience Christ at all. A church that seeks to manage its way through its own sin can hardly be said to have understood the resurrection. But the church that helplessly embraces the destruction of its own identity and still finds itself alive discovers a mission of conveying God's reconciliation to the broken world. It is simply impossible to make sense of a church that has perpetrated abuse, and nor should we try to do so. It is impossible to square the experience of resurrection with the insurance-led and solution-focused approach of the church towards abuse victims.

This is why the church finds itself at odds with itself, and paralysed by the issue of abuse. Like the resurrection, the experience of abuse, particularly physical or sexual abuse, is fundamentally transgressive and, for most individuals, cannot subsequently be incorporated into their narrative, but remains the event that is beyond meaning, and thus gives meaning to the rest of life. The church that recognises this should embrace victims of abuse, rather than seeking to distance itself from them in what appears to be a fear of their brokenness.

The practical outcome of this is that when a person discloses abuse in a church context, the response of church leaders, acting on behalf of the church, should be first and foremost to draw close to the victim. Recognising that this individual has had their personhood ruptured by an agent of Christ, the bishop should invoke Christ for the restoration of that personhood. In practice this means that instead of taking a managerial approach to dealing with the consequences of sin, church leaders should take a restorative approach, seeking the welfare of the victim above all. Their first and continuing question should be "What can I (and we as the church) do to help this individual? How can we identify with the damage that we have done to their personhood, and enable them to flourish in the days ahead?"

Those of us who walk with victims of abuse know that it is their own determination to flourish (or too often their belief that flourishing may never again be possible) that is uppermost in their minds and hearts, not financial recompense or legal resolution. The church, through its leaders, needs to find ways of saying from the outset, "The identity that was forced upon you by my colleagues in the church was untrue, and I am deeply sorry that we forced it upon you. From now on we will treat you with the dignity worthy of a child of God. What is more we hope and believe that you can flourish again, and we commit do everything within our power to making that possible."

In practice, of course, this rebuilding will not happen in a single meeting or event, any more than the original damage was caused in a single moment. What is needed is a restorative approach. It will require the intervention of skilled reconcilers (not mediators, since mediation implies fault on both sides.) The church may need to find imaginative ways of releasing whatever it is that the victim needs to flourish. Sometimes that may be information; sometimes it will be security in the form of guaranteed housing or sustained income. Sometimes it may involve public apology or other acts of humility. This will be time-consuming and humbling. It will require imagination. It may be costly in ways that insurers cannot comprehend. It will certainly require change from the church and its leaders.

One thing is certain – restoration is incompatible with business as usual. The goal throughout should be the flourishing of the victim, and if possible, the spiritual growth of the church and its leaders.

One of the distinctives of the church's response over the past ten years has been what might be described as "event apologies." When a fresh case of clergy wrongdoing comes to light, a bishop is sent out in public – often through the distancing medium of a press statement – to express how deeply sorry the church is for what happened, and how lessons will be learned. This cheap repentance turns the issue into a matter of procedure, and entirely bypasses the needs of the victim. Seldom if ever will a bishop meet the victim to kneel before them, or weep with them and their families, or ask what they need. To do so would be to acknowledge not just legal but more importantly spiritual indebtedness.

The number of impersonal event apologies issued by the church over the last ten years has meant that their value is exponentially diminished. Scripture tells us clearly that a cheap expression of apology without tangible acts of repentance is worthless. The church has looked in the mirror a thousand times, but has immediately forgotten what it looks like. If the leaders of the church want to truly represent their repentance for the church's sins, they may need to find far more potent symbols. What does a tangible act of repentance look like? Tearing of robes? Prostration? The wearing of ashes? At the very least surely it involves descending from the palace or bishop's croft to meet victims on their own terms to engage in deep and extended listening.

Those who are choosing how to respond on behalf of the church must recognise that just as the victim's efforts to rebuild and protect the value of their personhood will be lifelong, so the church's engagement with them on that journey must be lifelong too. This means that for victims of church abuse, reparation needs to be framed in terms of ongoing support, just is it is with other members of the church. In practice this means that the church should look to the victim's continuing needs, whether they are for counselling, housing, employment or finance. Reparation should be seen in terms of a stipend rather than a settlement. If this seems onerous it should be remembered that the extravagance with which the church chooses to anoint those whose identities have been utterly broken is the measure of the love it has for Christ. The question that church leaders need to ask in relation to victims of abuse is not how little can I pay them, but how much can I love them.

Andrew Graystone is a theologian and writer. As a journalist he broke the story of the abuse by John Smyth QC in the Iwerne network and in Africa. He continues to advocate for all victims of abuse.

Chapter 14

Wounded Leaders: Why Do Church Leaders Find It So Hard to Say #MeToo?

Andrew Graystone

We all have a lot to learn from the story of Bishop Greg Thompson. In March 2017 he resigned as Bishop of Newcastle, Australia, in the light of the Royal Commission on institutional responses to child sexual abuse. It's not that the commission had revealed that he was guilty of abuse. Quite the reverse. In the course of the inquiry Bishop Thompson had revealed that he himself was a victim of abuse, both by friends of his family when he was a child, and by a previous Bishop of Newcastle and another senior Church leader when he was a young adult.

The Bishop hasn't spoken much about the pressures that led to his resignation, but they included hundreds of abusive messages and also threats to himself, his family and his staff. For the sake of his physical and emotional health and that of his family he stood down in May 2017. He wasn't broken by his abusers. He was broken by his Church's failure to accept him as a victim.

The searchlight trained on the Church of England by the current Independent Inquiry into Child Sexual Abuse (IICSA) has revealed a culture of secrecy around all things sexual. It is notable that the pace of change has been set by the determination and persistence of survivors like Bishop Greg seeking justice, rather than by the resolve of senior leaders in the Church of England to find healing or even transparency. Former Archbishop Rowan Williams pointed out that a culture that demands dissembling around gay relationships also provides a place for abusers to hide. Those who aspire to leadership in the Church, but who have been victims of abuse, have been under great pressure to hide their victimhood in those same shadowy places.

A week before the February 2018 General Synod I published a little booklet called *We asked for bread but you gave us stones*. It is a collection of verbatim statements from people who have been victims of abuse in a Church context. In the week that followed the publication a number of synod members wrote to me to say that they too had been abused in various ways within the Church. Of course I immediately wrote back to offer what sympathy and support I could. In the current climate of disclosure I wasn't surprised to find Synod members saying "me too." What did surprise me was that none of those who wrote were bishops. To my knowledge at least a handful of serving bishops have also been victims of physical or sexual abuse. But with the exception of one, who was effectively forced by the media to speak about his abuse, none of them has chosen to speak publicly about their experience.

Why don't Church leaders choose to identify themselves as victims of abuse? What is it about the culture of the contemporary Church that prevents them from doing so?

You might easily ask why on earth they should. Perhaps one reason would be that the Church is struggling to understand and correct its own failures of care for the hundreds of people who have been abused by priests or other Church officers. In that context it would be immensely helpful to victims of abuse if those bishops and others who share their experience could stand with them. Of course abuse is a very personal business, and leaders and others have every right to deal with their victimhood within a very close circle of family or friends, if they choose to speak about it at all. If that were the only reason why senior leaders who have been abused chose to stay silent, I would understand. And yet there would seem to be other factors in the culture of the Church that hold leaders back from publicly owning their victimhood.

Those who identify themselves as victims own up to their own vulnerability – and it appears that we have made vulnerability unacceptable in Christian leaders. Although we may pay lip service to the notion of servant leadership, in practice we want leaders who are firm, resilient and decisive. 'Servant leadership' is a largely secular construct first aired in an essay in 1970 by Robert K. Greenleaf. It was quickly adopted by Church leaders, and even turned into a song by Graham Kendrick. Of course it has roots in the model of Jesus, who said that he had come to serve, and to give his life as a ransom for many; and before that it has theological roots in the Servant Songs of Isaiah. But it didn't make its way into Anglican thinking until the 1980s. An earlier generation of Church leaders wouldn't have recognised it.

Even when the language of servant leadership became current, only part of the model from Isaiah was adopted. The servant in Isaiah suffers viscerally; he has lent his back to the smiters and borne the scars of servanthood in his own body. He is a victim. By contrast we seem to want our "servant leaders" to be whole, robust, unscarred.

Bishop Thompson is a rare example of a senior Church leader who has identified himself as a victim. But he is far from the only Church leader to have been formed in a culture of abuse. There is no better example than the current Archbishop of Canterbury, who has revealed that he grew up in a largely dysfunctional family and went to schools where physical and sexual abuse was prevalent. At his first school, St Peter's, Seaford, several of his classmates were sexually abused by their teacher Christopher Jarvis, who is now serving a 13 year jail sentence. Welby then boarded at Eton, and spent his summer holidays at Iwerne camps, in the company of leaders like John Smyth, the disgraced QC whose beating of young men recruited at the camps is well-documented.

Archbishop Justin may or may not have been a victim himself as a child or a young adult. What is certain is that his formative years were spent in cultures where abuse was prevalent. Perhaps this accounts for his seeming paralysis in the face of the current crisis of abuse in the Church. As a pastor he appears to be deeply compassionate for victims of abuse, but as a leader he refuses to take decisive action. That may be because, having grown up in cultures of abuse, he simply fails to recognise it for what it is. Or it may be because he knows that to lead the Church effectively in dealing with the problem would expose the institutional abuses of the organisation that made him, and might even lead to its downfall. The dilemma is that if he fails to deal with the abusive culture of the Church it will certainly suffer the crashing loss of authority of the Roman Catholic Church in Ireland. As things stand we will look back on Justin Welby as the archbishop who missed the last best chance for the Church of England to save its remaining moral authority.

Meanwhile his fellow bishops, trained in safeguarding to within an inch of their mitres, have been content to allow Welby to squirm in the spotlight alone. The most managerially adept but theologically inept bench of bishops since the war have insisted that in dealing with abuse, authority in the Church of England must remain dispersed, whilst contrition must be centralised.

What is true for Archbishop Justin is true for a great many other Church leaders. The result of spending formative periods in abusive cultures varies from person to person. For some it sensitises them to abuse, making them particularly aware of power differentials. For others it may have the opposite effect. If bullying or abuse of power has become normative for you, it is difficult to identify it as a problem. Seeing and yet not seeing is a well-understood problem in cases of abuse. You may come to believe that resilience is a virtue; that high office requires a toughness that precludes vulnerability and requires you to suppress your personal pain.

Bishop Greg Thompson's experience suggests that members of churches can't cope with the idea that leaders are vulnerable. If you believe in a gospel that makes people whole, you might mistakenly expect that those who are furthest bought-in to that gospel should be the most whole. Church leaders who identify themselves as broken appear to be letting the side down. If the healing power of the gospel cannot be demonstrated in the people closest to God, the efficacy of the whole gospel project is called into question. That's the same reason why so many Church leaders won't generally own up to their depression, or their repressed sexuality, or their dependency on alcohol. Look behind the curtain and you may discover that, like the Wizard of Oz, your bishop is a mere mortal.

Somehow we have come to associate victimhood with weakness. It is as if we believe those who have been victims of abuse may have been too feeble to resist it – and if too feeble to resist, then certainly not tough enough for the rigours of Church leadership. We forget of course, that abuse is characterised by a disparity of power in which any normal child or vulnerable adult would have been overwhelmed. We forget that whilst the experience of being abused is devastating, the experience of recovering and rising above the abuse can demonstrate immense strength of character. By insisting that leaders seal off their darker experiences or keep them in the shadows, we diminish them as people, keeping them from experiencing the freedom and wholeness that they, and we, should enjoy. This is why so many bishops wait until retirement to express their true views on the Church's shadow-issues, or to be honest about their own doubts and pain.

Whether we like it or not, for many senior people in the Church, leadership is competitive. One friend who has been involved in training people for ordination said that they are amazed at how many young ordinands come to their initial training with a career path already mapped out. They seek jobs where they will be noticed, or that will be a springboard to preferment. In this climate, victimhood implies taint, shame, diminishment, disrespect. The leader who says they have been abused can expect to be treated like the last zebra in the pack, left for the hyenas to devour.

One mistaken perception is that men who have been abused by men may be unusually confused about their sexuality. Another common assumption is that victims of abuse are to blame for what happened to them. Perhaps the 15 year-old who was raped by a much older priest actually enjoyed the experience. Maybe he even goaded his abuser to assault him. Perhaps that so-called 'victim' is in fact guilty of placing sexual temptation in the way of a holy man. If victims are to blame for their own suffering, then a senior leader who discloses that they have been abused can expect to be held responsible. Instead of receiving the support of the community they may find themselves labelled as part of the problem. This is the experience of poor Bishop Thompson. In a perverse reversal, the abuser receives the support and sympathy of the Christian community, whilst the victim is shunned, lest they intentionally or unintentionally corrupt another good person. That's why so many victims of abuse speak about being re-abused by the response of the Church. Some even say that the rejection they experience when they disclose their abuse is worse than the original abuse. Wittingly or not, the Church by its actions has cast victims of abuse as the enemy; problems to be solved, or silenced, or bought off.

It doesn't have to be this way. Suppose we recognised that victimhood and its overcoming are a legitimate part of human experience and spiritual life. Suppose we reflect on our wounds as something that Christ shares, and even uses, in forming our relationship with God. Then we would recognise that victims are in fact our best theologians. Those whose humanity has been assaulted and robbed by people more powerful than themselves and yet fight for their survival and wholeness are making a potent statement about human worth and resilience. They have entered into the suffering of Christ. By the very fact that they fight for justice and a future they are saying that, whatever may be done to an individual, their humanity and dignity before God and the world remains intact.

Victims who own their victimhood are life-affirmers. They offer hope to a broken world, and a pattern of grace for a beaten Church. In Christian terms, they echo the deep theology of salvation, in which a wounded leader wins the world's future by triumphing over evil. Of course this is a radical reversal of the patterns of contemporary society. It is precisely this upside-down thinking that describes the Christian gospel and fuels the mission of the Church. The salvific power of wounds is so fundamental to Christian theology that we might go so far as to ask whether unbroken leadership is even possible. In her poem Hast thou no Scar? the Irish missionary Amy Carmichael, who spent years working with victims of abuse in India, asked, "Can he have followed far, who has no wound nor scar?" The visible scars of abuse are the stripes on the uniform of an officer of the Church. Instead of disqualifying the bearers from positions of authority, we need to ask whether anyone is qualified to lead in the Church without them.

Andrew Graystone is a theologian and writer. As a journalist he broke the story of the abuse by John Smyth QC in the Iwerne network and in Africa. He continues to advocate for all victims of abuse.

Chapter 15

Potential Safeguarding Solutions

David Greenwood (with MACSAS)

Fundamental improvement to our safeguarding laws is needed. It is to be hoped that the Independent Inquiry into Child Sex Abuse (IICSA) will recommend the changes which are summarised here:

1. Mandatory reporting – a new law should require professionals who work with children in 'Regulated Activities' to inform the LADO (Local Authority Designated Officer) or, in appropriate circumstances, Children's Services, where the professional knows or suspects child abuse, or has reasonable grounds for knowing or suspecting it. Failure to inform would be a criminal offence. Presently this is only guidance which is all too frequently ignored.

2. This legislation would foster a much stronger culture of abuse prevention as well as supporting and protecting mandated staff. In the absence of such a law those staff who do report are at present, by default, whistle-blowers with very little protection. Law can be a catalyst for behavioural and cultural change. The aim of the proposal is not to criminalise staff, but to support them when they are faced with the most challenging circumstances – concerns of potential or known child abuse. Being legally mandated to report removes an enormously challenging set of decisions staff are currently being asked to make.

3. Where the elements of the reporting obligation are met, there should be no exemption, excuse, protection or privilege granted to clergy for failing to report information disclosed in, or in connection with, a religious confession. It is questionable how this would be enforced against a sub-culture, such as the Catholic Church, which takes its orders from another central authority or has a countervailing belief structure. Undercover work by police officers could monitor the confessional.

4. The creation of a new independent statutory body to enforce basic standards of safeguarding, and to receive and deal with complaints

of child sex abuse (CSA) in all institutions which are responsible for the care of children.

5. This new statutory body would police and enforce minimum national standards of child safeguarding. It would have similar powers to the Health & Safety Executive. The HSE operates for the safety of workers; children are an even more vulnerable group. The absence of a powerful statutory body dedicated to their protection is a serious defect.

6. The issue of organisations avoiding regulation should be addressed. As unincorporated associations, bodies are merely groups of individuals which cannot be held accountable. They rely on goodwill to uphold a safeguarding function. The introduction of compulsory incorporation would establish a system of accountability.

7. The new independent statutory body should:

- Establish a register of relevant institutions that look after children.

- It would be an offence to look after children without being on the register.

- To be on the register institutions would have to introduce a corporate structure.

- Registered institutions would be forced to adhere to minimum safeguarding regulations.

- The body would have the power to prosecute regulated organisations for breaches of these regulations (similar to HSE prosecutions). Fines would be imposed.

- All complaints would be passed to the independent body by a receiving institution with a criminal sanction for failing to do so.

- The body would gather information from complainants, regulated institutions, and third parties. It would have the power to compel disclosure of material.

- It would liaise with and assist civil authorities such as the police and social services. It would ensure that the police and other statutory organisations take appropriate action within reasonable timescales. It would have the power to compel the police to investigate and refer cases to the Crown Prosecution Service.

- The body would investigate complaints using the balance of probabilities as the standard of proof. There would be no statute of limitations. It would have the power to make an award of compensation, similar to the Criminal Injuries Compensation Authority. It would decide the support to be offered to the complainant. A scheme would be established to provide adequate compensation for victims of child sex abuse, taking into account the effect on their quality of life and a series of relevant factors (as opposed to the rigid CICA system).

- Complainants would be allowed to take advice from lawyers, and a contribution towards legal costs would be awarded.

- The cost of the body's work, support, reparations and legal costs would be paid from a levy on the institutions, with those found culpable paying the costs of dealing with individual cases in which they are involved.

- The body would regularly report to the Government on its progress and, *inter alia,* the extent to which its activity promotes the UK's obligations under the UN convention on the Rights of the Child.

8. Proposed enhancements to the criminal justice system:
   - Judges should try cases without juries.
   - In cases where there is a jury, judges should give clear directions that they can find a defendant guilty if fewer than the present 10 jurors find guilt.
   - The training of judges should be more heavily informed by sessions with real life survivors who have experienced the prosecution process.

9. A review of the Charity Commission's powers should be initiated, to enable it to change charitable status when serious child safeguarding concerns are revealed.

10. Consideration should be given to the introduction of an offence of failing to protect a child from the risk of sexual abuse. Such a law was enacted in the Australian State of Victoria in 2015. Under the Victorian offence, in section 49C of the Crimes Act 1958, persons in authority in an organisation are required to protect children from a substantial risk of a sexual offence being committed by an

adult associated with that organisation, if they know of the risk. They must not negligently fail to reduce or remove a risk which they have the power or responsibility to reduce or remove.

11. There should be a review of the criminal offence of 'abuse of position of trust' under sections 16-24 of the Sexual Offences Act 2005. It should consider whether the existing categories of forbidden relationships with 17 and 18 year olds should be broadened. They could include, for instance, cases where the offender has an established personal relationship with the victim in connection with the provision of religious, sporting, musical, or other instruction to the victim. The categories as they currently stand are too narrow.

12. Finally, the implementation of an all-encompassing law requiring all statutes to be interpreted in a way that provides the maximum protection for children against harm, could be a step forward. This would require all institutions to rethink their relationship with the children for whom they are responsible.

This chapter draws on material gratefully acknowledged from Minister and Clergy Sexual Abuse Survivors (MACSAS).

David Greenwood *is Head of Child Abuse at Switalskis Solicitors.*

Chapter 16

What's Under the Bonnet?

Rosie Harper

How the Church responds to survivors, how we as individuals respond to survivors, is an infallible indicator of the sort of God we believe in.

Jesus knew this. He was fully aligned and there was never a gap between what he said about God and how he actually lived his life.

That gap is what people recognize very easily. They call it hypocrisy.

The strange thing about hypocrisy is that it is totally unintentional. No-one wakes up one morning and decides to be a hypocrite. It comes about when the drivers in your life turn out to be different from the ones you articulate.

A very basic example would be the church car park test. Imagine a sermon all about giving to the work of the church, or even giving to God. Standing at the door several people say; 'Good sermon. I quite agree, but things are rather tight for me at the moment.'

A glance at the church car park says it all. The Jag is parked next to the BMW. It's not even a matter of making a judgement. It's just how it is.

Another basic example: the Parochial Church Council (PCC) enthusiastically endorses a new emphasis on children's work. Without children there will be no future for the church. Let's have them joining us at the 10.00am service with some stories and activities in the Lady Chapel if they get restless.

Come Sunday morning little Freddie runs up and down the aisle and the self-same PCC members cannot restrain themselves; the usual "tut –tut", "why can't these parents control their children" comments pop out of their mouths. Although their heads have said the children are important, their hearts – what they really believe – still say it's their church and it only works for them if there is peace and order. They can't even help it. That's just how it is.

I am afraid that is what we are observing in the Church of England. I am weary beyond belief at the heartfelt apologies we are given. To begin with I thought they were genuine and waited for something to change. Then when nothing changed I thought they were cynical crocodile tears; and now I think that is just how it is. The apologies at a conscious level are perfectly genuine, but at a gut level, I have to conclude that the institution simply doesn't care. If I saw a cat run over by the side of the road I might or might not stop to help. I care a bit but not a lot. If I saw my mother run over by the side of the road I would move heaven and earth to help.

It is difficult therefore not to conclude, when we hear again and again that survivors are going to be put at the heart of the C of E response, and then nothing of the sort happens, that although they say they care – at a deeper level they do not. They simply do not care. That is why nothing better happens. It is what it is.

In his long *mea culpa* at the February 2018 General Synod, Peter Hancock (then lead bishop for safeguarding) admitted that in all the new work to improve the processes and structures of safeguarding they hadn't quite got round to the survivors, but that they would in due course. This made it very clear that devising ways to protect the institution was the main concern. The real, traumatically hurt human beings, many of them sitting in the chamber as he spoke, were an afterthought. When a person who has been abused says that feels like re-abuse they are right. When they say they are being treated with contempt they are right. Not because anyone is being wilfully evil, but because that is just how it is. When you care more about the Church than you care about the love of God then that is simply how you behave. It might be the whole institution behaving that way, or it might be individuals.

None of this is surprising. If you look at education, the Health Service, the media or business they have all had to put in a whole suite of checks and balances to try and ensure that they enact the values they say they hold. There is considerable clarity around accountability, but no process is perfect. It took families 20 years to get the NHS to take seriously the premature deaths of 450 elderly relatives due to the misuse of opioids at the Gosport War Memorial Hospital. Why would we think the Church was any different?

Indeed. This would be the end of the chapter if we believed that the Church was simply another institution. Many people think exactly that. You could choose to go to the golf club on Sunday morning, but you like the churchy thing. No problem. Whatever floats your boat.

The claim that Christians make, however, is far, far greater than that. The church is not the end but the means. Its role is as the delivery system for the Kingdom. The claim is that there is a living God who transforms our lives by the power of her love.

Christopher Lewis, the previous Dean of Christchurch, Oxford, famously replied to people who were getting anxious about the cathedral shop selling Harry Potter wands not to worry: "They don't work, you know."

People ask this of religion all the time. They suspect that when we pray we are actually talking to our imaginary friend, and that stories of divine intervention are just wishful thinking. They see all sorts of cruelty and injustice around the world that has its roots in religion and conclude that the world would be a better place without it.

As Christians we are asserting quite the opposite. Christian faith makes both individuals and communities better. There is another way to live, as demonstrated by Jesus, which does not meet violence with retaliation, nor hatred with anger. The whole point is that this way of being human is the way of love. Jesus was very explicit. You can test the authenticity of someone's claim to faith by looking at the quality of their relationships: "By this everyone will know that you are my disciples, if you have love for one another." (John 13.35)

If the car is not going forward it is probably because there is nothing under the bonnet.

So when the church responds without love, care, and reparation to the very people it has itself harmed, that is serious and potentially fatal. Basically it seems that the faith is not true. It doesn't change lives. Loving God does not result in loving your neighbour.

Those who say, "I love God," and hate their brothers or sisters, are liars; for those who do not love a brother or sister whom they have seen, cannot love God whom they have not seen. (1 John 4.20)

How do people of good faith and considerable natural pastoral instinct find themselves, in role, becoming the very sort of people that Jesus warned against?

There are various reasons. Firstly, it doesn't happen overnight. It happens through a series of little compromises made to stay the right side of the corporate line in order to progress. The general concept is that you keep your head down until you have enough power to make a difference. The trouble with that one is that every time you decide to keep silent you actually become the sort of person who doesn't rock the boat. Thus when you achieve the power you lack the character.

Secondly, everyone is trained within an inch of their lives to become hugely risk averse. Thus when a challenging case lands on the desk the first question becomes, 'what is the safe thing to do here?' rather than 'what is the right thing to do here?'

Thirdly, every diocesan bishop spends so much time wrestling difficult budgets to the ground that they buy into the poverty script. They genuinely think that we can't afford to make decent reparation, and that tuppence halfpenny is sufficient. They see no irony in preaching about the limitless and extraordinary love and generosity of God whilst failing to dip into the vast wealth of the Church of England to enable survivors to get their lives back on track.

But the big one underpins all this. If you spend your life, give your life, to the work of the Church, you can too easily end up mistaking the Church for God.

This can be seen by the current trend to talk about secularisation. It implies that God and the work of God is only to be found within the Church.

Once you have made this basic assumption, even when you do pretty murky things to cover up and protect the Church, you feel justified because you are actually protecting God.

That sort of God is a tiny, religious, defensive God and I think that is where we are.

The way the Church of England is responding to survivors exposes two utterly crucial fault lines. The first is the paucity of their vision of God. The second is a behaviour that implies that their faith is no faith at all.

Everyone is working very hard to produce new systems and more training and issue more apologies. It is hard to see this as anything other than moving the chairs around on the deck of the Titanic. Ireland used to have the highest church attendance in Europe. As safeguarding cases came to light and the Roman Catholic Church worked so hard to cover them up, attendance fell. It now has the lowest church attendance in Europe.

This is not a little local difficulty. This cuts to the heart of things. It is a test of the authenticity of the Christian faith.

The Rev Canon Rosie Harper is Vicar of Great Missenden and Chaplain to the Bishop of Buckingham.

Chapter 17

Cheap Grace and Child Abuse: Perhaps We Need Millstones Hanging Around a Few More Necks

Adrian Hilton

"Suffer the little children to come unto me, and forbid them not," said Jesus, "for of such is the kingdom of God" (Mark 10.14 Authorised Version). In this exhortation to childlikeness, to innocence and openness, to freedom and trust, there is no space for cruelty, abandonment or neglect; no tolerance of hypocrisy or pretension. Such abuse may be inflicted by commission or omission, for if we fail to prevent harm which we know is being wilfully inflicted; if we turn a blind eye to evil, we become complicit. And this includes historical child abuse where the victim is now an adult; and also vulnerable adults who are sexually exploited and spiritually harmed by those in whom they had placed a sacred trust. Influencing them toward evil, or inflicting evil upon them, has no place on the kingdom of God.

"And whosoever shall offend one of these little ones that believe in me, it is better for him that a millstone were hanged about his neck, and he were cast into the sea" (Mark 9.42 AV). The little ones here are children and all those lowly, weak, and vulnerable people who receive Jesus like children. To cause them to stumble morally or spiritually is worse than being drowned with your head jammed through the hole of a stone necklace, gasping for air as you're dragged down to the depths. Those who abuse the vulnerable and lead children astray will suffer a very particular apocalyptic judgment.

We all fall short, of course, because sin is our nature and depravity part of the human condition. And it's easy to fall for the pharisaical temptation of praying, "God, I thank thee, that I am not as other men are, extortioners, unjust, adulterers, or even as this publican" (Luke 18.11 AV). The Cross is the great leveller: penitent child-abusers may approach it and know the same mercy and forgiveness which has cleansed the spirits of sinners for two millennia. But this is costly forgiveness with a bloody sacrifice, not the cheap grace of a soundbite salvation which is devoid of the fear of God and oblivious to the remotest possibility of being drowned with a millstone around the neck.

"Shall we continue in sin, that grace may abound?" (Romans 6.1 AV). No, indeed: Christians are dead and buried with Christ; our minds are renewed; our lives are transformed by a divine relationship which orientates us to perfection and love. Salvation is cosmic: our slavery and sin are subject to a life-long process of self-sacrifice and perpetual re-recreation by a grace which costs us everything. An alternative justification was summarised by Dietrich Bonhoeffer: "The essence of grace, we suppose, is that the account has been paid in advance; and, because it has been paid, everything can be had for nothing. Since the cost was infinite, the possibilities of using and spending it are infinite." And so child abusers 'normalise' their behaviour, because children are there to be had, and the sin can quite easily be made to go away because Jesus is our substitute – no need for fear or trembling.

Cheap grace offends against the gospel, but nowhere near as much as a cheap episcopal cover-up. Both represent an abuse of ecclesial power, but the latter is arguably greater because the knowledge of evil is concealed by deceit or denied altogether, and that breaches faith and trust. By what understanding of the doctrine of forgiveness are abusers healed and reconciled while the young and vulnerable still suffer? By what apprehension of the image of God are abusers shielded from judgment and assured of the peace of pastoral compassion while their victims remain bound by years or decades of resentment, bitterness, self-loathing and deep hurt?

> Neil Todd and others subsequently reported that Ball repeatedly encouraged him to engage in 'spiritual' exercises involving nakedness and cold showers. In September 1992 Ball suggested that Todd should agree to be beaten while naked so that his body should "bear the marks"...
>
> There was a common theme involving nakedness. The informants referred to matters such as stripping naked and caressing, being asked to masturbate in front of Ball and sharing the same bed as Ball. There were further suggestions of "genital contact" and assault or flagellation.
>
> ..."He said it was God's will."
>
> (*An Abuse of Faith: The Independent Peter Ball Review,* Dame Moira Gibb, 2017)

Neil Todd attempted suicide twice, apparently trying to purge his memory of the 'spiritual' exercises and the naked beatings inflicted so that his body might bear the marks of Christ.

"The abuse was varied. The worst of it was mental abuse. Obviously there was a component of sexual abuse. But basically it was mind games and controlling behaviour," he explained shortly before his third suicide bid, by which he finally managed to end his anguish.

How can priests in the Body of Christ sexually abuse children one day, and get on their knees the next and somehow 'know' that God has forgiven them; that their 'slate has been wiped clean'? Why do so many bishops collude in this cheap grace when the abused find it so hard to forgive the snares and traps that were set for them – even to the point of suicide? When the violated are hanging in psycho-spiritual limbo; when relationship has not been restored by humility, sorrow, repentance and communion on the part of the abuser; who can dare to proclaim 'forgiven in the name of Jesus' over those who have offended against the Lord's little ones?

"Bind up the wounds of those who have been hurt, and in your mercy make us whole", says the Church of England's new liturgy for the abused. It's hard for them to pray for healing when they are left hanging on a cross between rape and review. How long must they wait for justice and redress? How can we plead for their wounds to be bound when not enough millstones have been hung around not enough necks?

As I write, there are a number of serving bishops who stand accused of turning a blind eye to chronic sexual abuse by other members of the clergy: there are allegations of collusion, manipulation and complicity in cover-up for reputational preservation, and even of cover-up of the cover-up. And the evidence is persuasive and damning. Why is a long-dead bishop like George Bell so readily thrown under a bus over one single, uncorroborated allegation, while living and serving bishops are shielded by a 'one-year rule' for a complaint to be made against them? What possible incentive do they have for consenting to dispense with that arbitrary rule when it would mean a discomfiting investigation into their failures and shortcomings? How may one hold diocesan bishops to account during their term of office when the relevant metropolitan bishop refuses to act?

The answer, of course, is that one cannot: they are kings in their dioceses, masters of their parishes, overseers of all boards and councils responsible for ministry and mission. They are immune from external investigation, shielded from the arrows of oversight, and guarded by the episcopal sword of sanctity. And this is apparently immutable, as the recent report to Synod by the National Safeguarding Steering Group made clear:

Whatever changes may be made in safeguarding operational structures now and in the future, the accountabilities and responsibilities of bishops, priests and Church officers will remain unchanged. No safeguarding structure, whether internal or external, can take over the core role in mission and ministry of bishops and priests. They need to continue to carry out these duties safely and ensure that others do so too.
(GS 2092, June 2018, para.71)

And so the inaction and collusion will continue, and justice delayed will be compounded by vacuous leitmotifs of 'zero tolerance' of abuse and abundant prayers for the abused. It's difficult to rationalise this, other than perhaps to conjecture that some bishops no longer believe in the possibility of apocalyptic millstones; that judgment and hell have been relegated to la-la land. Journalist Rod Liddle shared an interesting insight about episcopal belief in eternal torment in one of his columns:

It's not just the Catholics, of course. A few years ago I was chatting to a very senior Church of England bishop about the notion of Hell. Does Hell exist, I asked the chap, ingenuously. "Oh Rod, don't be so bloody stupid." Ah, OK. Then what about God? He looked a bit conflicted at this question, mused for a while and then wobbled his hand about a bit. Maybe, maybe not.
(*Sunday Times,* 1 April 2018).

A 'senior bishop' who doesn't believe in hell is perhaps no longer surprising, but one who casts doubt upon the existence of God is a little worrying. Why should clergy not use children for their sexual gratification when the Day of Judgment never comes? Why should bishops not conspire in cover-up when that which is unknown shall never be made known? What need personal holiness or the Christian virtue of forgiveness when it's all just a self-therapeutic delusion?

Or is it that somewhere deep down there's a belief that child abuse isn't really as bad as Jesus made it out to be, and it's all being absurdly over-hyped in an era obsessed by 'Safeguarding'? As one person wrote to me:

I attended a boys' public school similar to the one which [the abuser] attended a decade earlier. The kind of thing which [he] got up to was not uncommon among the masters, nor was it at other such schools which I knew about. By the boys it was regarded as a bit of a joke. You will find this attitude very accurately reflected in Alan Bennett's *The History Boys* (I'm surprised it hasn't been banned). If you had told my contemporaries that one day boys would claim substantial sums of money for these attentions and make it the most important thing in their life, they simply wouldn't have believed you.

...To find that somebody who you thought loved you for yourself when he only (?) wanted to get into your pants (though the two objectives are not irreconcilable) could be devastating and totally disillusioning. But such experiences are common to the human condition. To what extent should they be in the public forum, any more than your parents, your partner, your friend letting you down should be? And to what extent should we seek financial compensation for any of these disappointments?

There's no apparent understanding that children are harmed by abuse in different ways, no appreciation of the special place Jesus has for children, and no apprehension of judgment involving millstones. Human resilience is variable, of course, but the reason Jesus is particularly concerned about his little ones is because to offend against them profoundly affects the formation of their identities – it harms their self-perception and capacity for relational intimacy. What image of God can the abused child have when the priest, who is supposed to reflect and radiate the divine image, abuses his power and infects innocence with lust and perversion? How can these little ones ever forgive God when his visible and identifiable representative on earth whispered that this 'special love' was all God's will?

Many do, of course, but a great many more do not. In one gathering of 60 survivors of clergy abuse, when asked how many of them attend church, just two hands went up. The story is mentioned in one of the Church of England's booklets on this subject: *The Gospel, Sexual Abuse and the Church: A Theological Resource for the Local Church* (Church House Publishing, 2016, page 30). It reminds us: "The call to repentance is a call to turn to life and share in God's kingdom, not a summons to endless punishment inflicted by others or even oneself" (page 27), and it refers to those millstones which will be hung around the necks of those who put 'stumbling blocks' before those little ones (Matthew 18.6). But there is no theological exposition: it segues straight into a comment on Psalm 96.13 AV: "God's judgement is good news because it promises the restoration of justice in human relations, without which there can be no peace."

In the church's subsequent resource, *Forgiveness and Reconciliation in the Aftermath of Abuse* (Church House Publishing, 2017), the theological focus is exactly as the title suggests, despite observing: "for some survivors there is real anger that the church seems so preoccupied with forgiveness in the aftermath of abuse, when the focus should be on justice" (page 10). No one is saying there should be no mercy or can be no reconciliation, "For all have sinned, and come short of the glory of God" (Romans 3.23 AV): it is simply that there's a feeling that wiping the slate clean should be rather more costly.

Cheap grace is not only the root of 'normalising' child grooming and exploitation; it is also a seed of precipitate restoration – of the sort which, rather than cleansing hearts and renewing minds, becomes a cloak behind which sexual abuse is re-imagined and realised cyclically, because it isn't really abuse at all; at least not serious abuse. And the 'victim' isn't really a victim; they consented so readily to flattering words and preludes of adoration. It all seemed so genuinely friendly and heartfelt; the mutual trust and commitment to flourishing. Only years later does it become a matter of blame and deep shame. The Bishop of Chichester, Martin Warner, was asked by the BBC in October 2017: "If a bishop urged a member of the clergy who was in contact with a victim of abuse to stay quiet and not go to the police or the media, would you consider that to be cover-up?" The Bishop responded: "Yes I would – by today's standards, in terms of our practice today, that would immediately be the trigger for disciplinary action."

Which raises the question of why yesterday's standards – just 15 or 20 years ago – were so deficient. We are talking about the rape and abuse of children and the systematic cover-up of that abuse. When in two millennia of Church history was that ever acceptable? What manner of bishop is more concerned with institutional reputation than with justice for the vulnerable and oppressed? Do they feel more for the sadistic abuser than the raped child? Do they have more respect for clergy who gratify themselves with children than they have for their wounded victims? Aren't millstones the same yesterday, today and forever?

As the Church of England crawls toward greater repentance and deeper holiness – acknowledging not only that it got things badly wrong historically but continues to do so – it might help to inspire reconciliation in the Church and rebuild trust with the world if remorse were a little more public and penance rather more severe. Eternal millstones are for the Lord to dispense, of course, but perhaps we might see a few more self-imposed temporal millstones – of the sort worn with sincere humility by John Profumo and Jonathan Aitken, for example – which speak far more eloquently than crafted statements for media consumption. It's also worth remembering that one of the qualifications for being a bishop is having a good reputation in the world: "Moreover he must have a good report of them which are without; lest he fall into reproach and the snare of the devil" (1 Timothy 3.7 AV). It is one thing to learn privately from past safeguarding failures; quite another to be trusted by outsiders with the care of their children. People within and without want to see a safeguarding structure to help guard bishops from disgrace and the possibility they might fall into the devil's trap. Isn't another Erastian millstone a little lighter to wear than the eternal one?

Dr Adrian Hilton *is a theologian, political philosopher, educationalist and author. He lectures in the UK and the US.*

Chapter 18

The Unworthy Inheritor:
The Church of England and the
Memory of George Bell

Peter Hitchens

The image of a chimpanzee capering across a marble floor clutching a Ming vase often comes to mind these days. We wait for the inevitable crash and clatter, and wonder where we put the glue. A society such as ours is rich in inherited treasures whose inheritors neither know nor care how important they are and seem unfitted to look after them for the next generation. Usually, these legacies are material – unspoiled landscapes, lovely buildings, venerable institutions, picturesque traditions, or simple high standards maintained in a world of low ones.

In some of these matters, the Church of England is a reasonably good steward. Its churches and cathedrals are reasonably well-maintained and not too badly spoiled by pestilential modernisers. Its choral music, at least in the great centres of excellence such as the major cathedrals and the greater Oxbridge chapel choirs, is still kept to a high standard.

But this creditable performance only serves to hide a much deeper dereliction. I like to describe the C of E as a brilliant attempt to dissolve dogmatic differences in beauty. I reject the constant dismissals of Anglicanism as too vague and feeble to be taken seriously as a religious force. On the contrary, I think that it was a work of genius to instil into almost every mind in England the glories of the Authorised Version of the Bible and the Book of Common Prayer. Heard regularly at Matins and at Evensong, often accompanied by matching wonders of architecture and music, these feats of poetry brought twenty generations of men and women closer to God than they would ever otherwise have been. And they passed on what they had learned in lives of patience, forbearance, modesty and cheerfulness, the characteristics of the society I remember dying all around me in my childhood.

We heard, and we read, and we did what we were commanded to do, as far as possible, in daily life. It was "a serious place on serious earth". It did not possess the grandiose intransigence, or even the supposed intellectual coherence, which Evelyn Waugh came to admire in the Roman Catholic Church. But it was certainly not stupid or thoughtless, and it did not lack force. Nor was it, as some Americans continue to imagine, and some Roman Catholics still jeer, a state Church bowing to the government.

And one of the greatest examples of its genuine power was in the life of George Kennedy Allen Bell. I have met a man who knew George Bell and worked for him, and before he died, he utterly confirmed my own impression of Bell, gained only from reading about him. This particular witness, later a clergyman, had served in the Royal Navy during the war, had seen serious action and been mentioned in dispatches, three words I have always wished I could one day put after my name, but never will. He principally admired Bell for his courage. He believed that Bell was Mr Valiant-for-Truth, John Bunyan's most admirable character in *The Pilgrim's Progress*. It was Mr Valiant-for-Truth who said at the moment of his death these most moving words, "I am going to my Father's; and though with great difficulty I am got hither, yet now I do not repent me of all the trouble I have been at to arrive where I am. My sword I give to him that shall succeed me in my pilgrimage, and my courage and skill to him that can get it. My marks and scars I carry with me, to be a witness for me that I have fought His battles who now will be my rewarder." Bunyan then added, "So he passed over, and all the trumpets sounded for him on the other side."

If you are of my generation, this plain soldierly English burns like fire on the tongue. I suspect it would have done so for Bell as well. He knew what valour was, and what it cost. Three of his brothers had died in the Great War. He was himself an accomplished poet, and a great recogniser of true poetic genius in others. So when the moments came in his life when he must be tested, he drew himself up with a full heart and did what he believed God meant him to do. He espoused unpopular causes, because he believed them to be right, most notably that of German Jewish refugees being stupidly rounded up by the Churchill government in 1940, and that of opposing the RAF's deliberate bombing of German civilians in their homes later in the same war. And he paid for it, both in cruel public mockery, cold shoulders and, very likely, in being denied the post of Archbishop of Canterbury which he would greatly have adorned. Is this not what Christians are meant to do? And how would we see it done, in a peaceful kindly England without the stake or the rack, but with its other more subtle ways of punishing the heretic and the man of principle? Here, in one man and in one moment, the very essence of Anglicanism, as it once was, was expressed.

I have come to the point this way because I think everyone who is remotely interested will know about the ancient, anonymous, uncor-roborated allegation of child sexual abuse made against George Bell more than 50 years after his death. They will know of the George Bell Group's forensic dissection of the charges. They will know of the sub-sequent forensic probe into the botched, one-sided and inadequate in-vestigation of the charges by the Church bureaucracy. They will have read the coldly devastating report by Lord Carlile, QC. Lord Carlile, to put it mildly, cast grave doubt on the strength of the accusations and the quality of the investigation.

They will also know of the Church of England's curious rush to make the original allegations public, though (as a senior bishop sub-sequently admitted) they were not sure they were true; and of the strange press release issued by the Church which managed to give the impression that Bell was guilty as charged, without actually saying so.

These are all bad enough. Worse still was the Archbishop of Canterbury's behavior. After all, this was over and Bell's defenders at last allowed themselves a moment of joy at the vindication of this great man. The Archbishop was not going to be deflected by anything so trivial as evidence and due process, or a report by one of the coun-try's most distinguished lawyers. No, for him, a "significant cloud" still hung over George Bell's name, and it is very hard to see what would shift that cloud from Justin Welby's portion of the moral sky.

If an unproven allegation against a dead person means a permanent taint of suspicion in all cases, where does that leave any of us, includ-ing him, if allegations are made against us once we are in the grave and not there to defend ourselves? So the Stalinoid stripping of Bell's name from buildings and schools continued. Within days, another startling thing happened. For two years, a serious effort had been made to urge anyone else with a complaint against George Bell to come forward. A special telephone line was provided. Lord Carlile had likewise sought to hear from any others with such allegations. During that time, the case had received immense local and national publicity. But not a sin-gle further complaint had been received.

Yet soon after Lord Carlile's report devastated the first charge against Bell, a new allegation against him was suddenly said to have been made. But the Church, previously so keen to share details of charges against Bell with the press, recoiled like a salted snail or an affronted maiden aunt when asked to say what this new allegation was. The police, to whom the matter was passed, shortly afterwards dropped the case, declining to say anything about it. The Church, told of this, simply refused to discuss the matter, claiming a need for confidentiality, though nobody sought to identify the new accuser.

And here is the point of all this background and foreground. The initial public smearing of George Bell's name, while foolish and rushed and, to my mind, inexcusable, is in a way understandable. It could have been seen then as part of the Church's attempt to get a grip on the problem of child abuse. There has been much wrongdoing in the Chichester diocese, not all of it promptly or thoroughly dealt with. An ignorant person who knew nothing of George Bell might have thought that it would be good for the Church to act sternly against someone, anybody, even a dead prelate.

But nobody has that excuse now. The defenders of George Bell have reminded the country and the Church of the forgotten reasons for his high standing. They have shown the modern world an old-fashioned Englishman, unaligned with any modern Church faction or fashion, a man of simple self-sacrificing courage, such as we are asked to be. That is the core of his reputation. Mr Welby seems to think that Bell could still be a bit of a great man as well as a child abuser, perhaps along the lines of Eric Gill, whose sculptures are still great works of art despite his revolting sexual behaviour. This is ridiculous. Bell's greatness lies in his display of real virtue, his insistence on telling the truth even, nay, especially when it would damage him to do so. How can this be compatible with the filthy, lying betrayal of a little girl alleged against him? If he really did do both, then the miserable crime utterly sweeps away the claim to be Mr Valiant-for-Truth.

No, I think the problem is that, even when it is explained and described to them, the leaders of today's Church of England neither understand nor value George Bell's plain sort of Christianity. They are glad to be rid of it because they believe in something else. I am not sure what it is, but I suspect I would not much like it if I did. Some may remember John Betjeman's 1965 TV play, *Pity About the Abbey*. It was about people who could see nothing really wrong with removing Westminster Abbey to make way for a new motorway scheme. It was only a mild caricature of reality, in a world where it could be seriously suggested that a by-pass might be built across Christ Church Meadow in Oxford. It is the same sort of thing. They do not know what they have, or care whether they pass it on to others yet to come, who may (one still hopes) have more sense than they do.

Peter Hitchens *is an author and columnist for the* Mail on Sunday.

Chapter 19

Olive Tree

Cliff James

At the foot of the Mount of Olives, they say, is the Garden of Gethsemane ... Gethsemane was significant to Peter; he made it significant to others. There is a house in the South Downs of England, a bishop's house, where the Garden of Gethsemane was made manifest. (From Life As A Kite*)*

Grey is a saint –

shin-deep in snail shells
and stories of sand;
his old toe must taproot
the ancestors of god,
tampers the silence.

Grey is a shrine –

of dead seas and bread-stones,
a hand-cupped supper of nights
overflowing with watch,
with drip-drip cicadas
singing of keys.

Grey is a secret –

robed in sackcloth
and crook: you can climb
his contortions for a shekel,
less if you slip through the iron,
ride the horsehair bare.

Grey is a sacrament –

in the inner sanctum

of a cloven bole, swept bald
and braced on four hooves
for a glorious ascension;
bray the revelation.

Grey is transcendent –

both fossil and flame,
lightning and trident
roaring millennia in a whisper
of leaves taken and eaten,
sometimes a flash of black seeds.

Grey is immanent –

can never be unseen,
his seam runs deep in the desert.
Ring him with railings, carve names
on the bough: he slouches centuries,
grazes under-bone, the buried unborn

Cliff James is a writer and poet.

Chapter 20

Trust, Hope and a Reluctant Divorce

Jo Kind

I trusted my vicar, why shouldn't I? I had known him since I was 6 years old; he was a friend of my parents; his preaching and teaching brought me to a faith in God; hundreds of others came to faith through him; he was seen to cast out demons in Jesus' name, for goodness sake; he was heading for a senior appointment in the Church of England – why shouldn't I trust him?

At the age of 23, I went to work for my vicar. I was a young graduate, eager to begin my first full-time job and equally eager to serve God in the church where I'd grown up and been so happy. When my vicar told me during my job interview that he had received medical advice to take his clothes off as much as possible to help with a low libido, and that if I would agree to him being naked in the office where we worked, he would see it as a blessing from God – why shouldn't I trust him? My trust in him was so deep that I was unable to comprehend that he could cause me any harm. It could be said that I gave my consent; my consent was in no way informed and was inextricably linked to my spiritual aspiration to serve God.

I was harmed. I was harmed by having a man the age of my father, indecently exposing himself to me most days of the week over a period of nearly two years; I was harmed by the silence, complicity and responsibility that he imposed on me; I was harmed by a subconscious inner conflict which remained suppressed for many years; I was harmed by the colossal amount of chocolate I consumed to repress the terror and isolation which I couldn't allow myself to feel at the time. How could I even think to escape? Wasn't I working for a man of God and enabling him to reach others for Christ? How could I even think to question?

So...
So, you let me in on your secret.
So, you made me feel quite privileged.
So, you made me feel important, yet in doing so made me worthless.
So, everyone else had the good you, and I had the bad you.

If the bad you wasn't happening, then the good you couldn't function,
    couldn't save souls, couldn't teach and guide.
And so, I accepted the bad you to help the people who liked the good you.
You made out it was to serve God, a gift from Him, but NO!
And I just had to serve you, keep silent for the bad you; nothing about God, just
all about you.
(15 October 2011)

I kept silent for over 19 years; I locked away the memory of my vicar so that I didn't even consider it, somewhere where the hurt would only seep into my life rather than flooding into it. Clever, eh? And then somehow the dam burst. In November 2008, I found myself aged 42 and for the first time disclosing the abuse to another vicar and his wife – lovely, well-intentioned people who had also been hurt by the knowledge of what had occurred in the vicarage where I had worked with my vicar and where they now lived. That was nearly ten years ago, when I still trusted the Church of England to respond well.

I trusted the C of E. Why shouldn't I? I didn't really know what I was doing when I reported what had happened, apart from needing to share the sudden and new revelation that my vicar's behaviour had been terribly wrong, that it was already known about by many, and please could the pressing sense of responsibility I had experienced for nearly two decades now be shared with them? Please could the wrong be brought out into the light and seen for what it was at last?

I trusted that the church where all this had occurred would want light to be shed on past wrongs. I was told that my courage in reporting was offering a chance to my ageing vicar to repent and for the church in question to be set free from the hold of the past. Please would I write about it in two letters and the vicar would be challenged?

And then, like so many victims of abuse before and after me, I was told that the bishop would see me if I wanted, that he would be praying for me, and that if the matter was to be taken further and the vicar challenged, I would need to make an official complaint. As a victim of abuse making a disclosure, I was acutely vulnerable – I am not unusual in that – so much for my hope of shared responsibility. In an instant I felt isolated. I expected that someone would follow up with care and suggestions of what next. I waited for that to happen, I waited for help, I thought that something would be done – surely it would be done, because I had supposedly given the vicar the opportunity to repent whilst he was still in his mid-70s and what could be more important than that? I gave up any expectation of help or action. So many still do – we report, we are listened to, we give information freely, we are told we are courageous and have done nothing wrong and then ... zilch. Trust knocked.

Two years and four months passed, and in March 2011 the dam, of now barely suppressed hurt, broke again and I found myself writing to the bishop through a mess of tears; writing to him enclosing the letters I had written previously, asking him what could be done, asking him what should be done? During the next 6 years my trust in the Church of England's systems and officers eroded to nothing. How can trust be retained when it is treated with at worst disdain and at best off-handedness? How can trust be retained when promises are repeatedly broken and when pertinent and important questions are repeatedly ignored? How can trust be retained when the sexually abusive behaviour of the vicar is explained away by the notion that "at times he sunbathed without clothes in my presence"? In England? In February? Indoors? Trust broken!

So, what of hope? I retained it for some time and still do on occasion. At the start of 2014, I expressed it in this way:

> I love the Anglican Church.
> It has always been my home; the place where I learnt about a living God and developed a deep relationship with him; the place where my family belonged – where we had friends, where we would take our friends.
> The safest place I knew.
> I love the Anglican Church even though it is the place where I experienced the deepest pain and the most devastating harm.
> I thought that I hated the Anglican Church – that the trauma of the abuse and of reporting it was too much.
>
> It would be easier to hate it; it would be easier to walk away from it because it is no longer safe, and to advise others to do the same, but I cannot – I still have hope.
> I fear for my Church because it struggles to seek out truth. It would rather fix on what it does well than work out where it has gone wrong.
> I fear for the Church I love because it binds up some of the broken-hearted but then leaves them with festering bandages.
> I fear for the Church that hurt me because it doesn't have the courage to seek out those whose harm has led to hate and whose pain has silenced them.
>
> I call on my Church, on the Church that I love, to shatter dynamics that allow the hurt to continue; to have the strength to act like Jesus – to stop in its tracks and listen, to act with courageous compassion, to overturn tables if necessary, to walk with those who are broken, to give hope to those whose lives have been shattered...to restore life.
> (3 January 2014)

At this point I had tried to withdraw from any contact with the diocese where the abuse had taken place. Trying to communicate with people whom I felt had completely broken my trust was too re-trau-matising and harmful. I was deeply hurt that members of the leader-ship of the church, along with the bishop, had held a service of repen-tance and prayer for healing without inviting me. I was deeply hurt by confidentiality breaches. I was deeply hurt by lengthy periods of silence without promised communication. I felt fobbed off and worth-less and as though I was making a mountain out of a mole-hill. I felt, and I still feel, that it was easier for the church in question to focus on my persistence and to perceive it as absence of healing, than it was to focus on the truth of the sexually deviant and abusive behaviour of the vicar and its effect on the people and life of the Church.

Maybe if people focus on the victim's response to being abused and the victim's behaviour, they can somehow protect themselves from having to view the perpetrator as anything other than a great person of God who had some unfortunate flaws. I am unable to find that pro-tection. I know and have fully faced the reality of what this man did and how it devastated parts of my life, and yet I still must hold the reality that he helped many people and had a seemingly successful ministry.

Two thousand and fifteen was the year of the CDM (a complaint un-der the Clergy Discipline Measure). It took the whole year and nearly took my sanity with it. If nothing else, my letter to a broken Church is to request that it suspends the use of the Clergy Discipline Measure (2003) for any complaints made about sexual abuse or exploitation. The Measure does not provide the safety of set timeframes; it offers more support to the Respondent than it does to the Complainant; it lacks transparency and accountability in its recording of penalties on the Archbishops' List. It is dependent on bishops, most of whom lack the time or skill to fully understand and implement Canon Law, and who are put in the ludicrous position of having to investigate and pass judgement on colleagues. The CDM didn't break me or my marriage, nor did it take my sanity, but it came precariously close to doing all three. And to survive the CDM process as a complainant I had to sus-pend hope in the C of E, to have a healthy and conscious uncoupling:

Break-off point, or Ça suffit C of E
No more
No more waiting for things that won't arrive
No more asking
No more putting myself at risk
No more

I am entitled to peace of mind but will find it another way
I am entitled to be treated with fairness but will seek that elsewhere
I am entitled to the respect of others for I have done no wrong in this

I will not be silenced and brushed away
I will challenge but I will not ask
I will not be humoured
I will not give up but I give up on them
They have not broken me

I need nothing from them
They may listen to me but I don't need that
They may seem to respect me but I don't need that

The silence of those who lead speaks louder and with more clarity than any words they may say

I am not broken but they have broken my trust

I will walk tall and stay strong and my words will replace their silence
I will continue to speak truth with fairness and with my own hope
Hope in the Church?
No more.
(22 November 2015)

2008–2018? Loss of trust, abandonment of hope and a very reluctant but necessary divorce from the Church I love.

Jo Kind *is a survivor, MACSAS (Ministers and Clergy Sexual Abuse Survivors) committee member, and a volunteer support worker.*

Chapter 21

The Power of Purple

Janet Lord

Sundays were always special at home. In the 1970s, the shops weren't open, and it was a day for reflection and prayer. My brother and I weren't allowed to play outside, we had to stay in and read, or play quiet indoor games. Some of that was normal in lots of households; but in our house, it was even more special, because my lovely dad was a vicar. I absolutely loved being the vicar's daughter. My mum was more reserved than I was, and not too happy about being the traditional 'vicar's wife'. Besides, she had a full time and responsible job of her own. So there was a space for me – a space I happily and willingly moved into throughout my childhood and teenage years.

On Sundays, I would always get up early, and help my dad prepare for the day ahead. Together, we would cut Mother's Pride bread into squares for the 8am communion service at the local church school. Dad would go off to the first Holy Communion of the day, and I stayed at home, ready to help make his breakfast when he came in and then to go off with him to our church. I loved the ritual of getting the church ready for the service – of putting the celebrant's robes ready, lighting the candles, slotting the hymn board numbers in the board, and acting as sacristan, reverently preparing the wafers and wine.

I was also a chorister, and I'd enjoy putting on my blue cassock, my surplice and my RNCM badge, ready for the processional hymn. After the service, members of the PCC would come back to the vicarage for coffee. At Christmastime, as well as coffee, we'd have Christmas cake and portions of Stilton cheese – we always had a full Stilton, and dad would hollow it out a bit with a serving spoon and pour port into it for a treat. Then we'd all sit round having coffee and chatting. At Easter, it was even more exciting – in those days, the Easter collection was the vicar's to keep as part of his stipend. Members of the congregation knew that and gave generously. And so the Easter Offering was counted out ceremoniously and excitedly by the whole family and the church treasurer.

Those memories are very vivid, and show how being the vicar's daughter was a key component of my identity. My faith was important to me; I was a pious little girl, and a slightly less pious but still earnest young teenager. Although I was sometimes teased at school for being a 'goody two-shoes' I didn't really mind. Religion and the Church were part of who I was.

All that changed when I was about 14. My dad had gone on a retreat – he was very stressed and needed a rest. He never really came back to the parish from that rest. For years, he had had a relationship with a woman he had met at a church conference, and was in love with her. He hated living the double life that he did – as a parish priest with a family, but also as a man who was deeply in love with someone other than his wife. He left the family home, knowing that as well as leaving us he was deserting his house, his parish, the parishioners, and probably the Church.

That was devastating enough for me. But despite my despair, my sadness in missing my lovely dad who I adored, I felt that I had the Church, my faith and my religion to comfort me. How wrong I was. The tabloid newspapers got hold of the story, and we made the Sunday headlines. Divorce was much more rare in the early 1970s, and vicars were supposed to be models of piety and goodness. Certainly, they were not supposed to leave their family, vicarage and parish because of an extramarital relationship. The phone never stopped ringing. We couldn't go to school as we were hounded by the press – we were pariahs. My mum took me and my brother away to Chester, to stay with my granny, to avoid the papers and to try and protect us. But in fact, it was in Chester that we were very far from safe.

One morning in Chester, we had a message that the bishop wanted to see me and my brother, to ask how we were and to check that we were coping. All I really knew about Bishop Whitsey was that he was hugely important. He signed himself with his first name and a cross, 'Victor +'. I thought that was a sign of power. And of course it was. I can't emphasise enough what a big deal going to see the bishop was – we were taken to buy new clothes, and to have haircuts, all in his honour. I knew that I had to be on my best behaviour and that this meeting mattered – it might affect my dad's future in the Church, and whether or not we would have a family home any more. I was terrified of being homeless, and I knew that the Church would throw us out of the vicarage where I had grown up if my dad didn't remain as parish priest. I was a tad surprised that the bishop didn't want to see my mum as well as me and my brother, but as he was all-knowing, all-powerful, I didn't ask any questions.

The great day arrived. I remember arriving at the Bishop's Palace in Chester, which is situated in an imposing square. We came from a disadvantaged parish and I wasn't used to such opulence. Parish priests' stipends weren't enough to provide a luxurious lifestyle. As we went up the steps and into the palace, we were overawed by the huge fragrant flower arrangements and antique furniture. I felt very small and insignificant, and I suspect my little brother felt even more so.

Again I was surprised that my brother and I were asked to see the Bishop separately. I was terrified – I didn't know what I would say. The Bishop was very tall, very big, very purple. He said that physical comfort was the best kind. He said 'suffer the little children to come unto me'. And then he abused me.

I was bewildered, confused, hurt, worried. I had tried to shy away from being comforted physically, but he was a big man, and this was difficult for me. I was so conscious that this purple monster held my family's future and our house in his gift, and I knew I couldn't do anything to upset that. I didn't tell anyone. I didn't know who I could have told, anyway. The bishop was all seeing, all powerful, and I had thought, all loving.

That was the beginning of the end of my relationship with the Church of England. As I write this, I look back and see that confused girl, who was already hurting, who was looking for comfort and for love, but who instead found abuse, a sexual initiation based on power and exploitation, and a stripping away of her identity. I didn't tell anyone at all for many, many years. Before he died, a few years ago, my brother and I – almost accidentally – shared the fact that we had both been abused that day. For my brother, this abuse had majorly coloured his adult life. He followed Whitsey's career carefully and breathed a sigh of relief when Whitsey died; the spectre was put to rest. For me, the white male hegemony of the Church had let me down, used its power to destroy me and had undermined the integrity of my identity: as a young woman, as a person of faith, a servant of God and the Church. That's what I felt, though I wouldn't have been able to articulate it like that then.

First, the overwhelming massive purpleness of Whitsey had started to destroy who I was. Secondly, the fact that the Church had not provided anywhere for me to go to report or talk about the abuse meant that I turned on myself. I sought out love and understanding in other places, and opened myself up to more abuse and abusers. Finally, even when, as adults, my brother and I did disclose to each other, this disclosure by chance was heard by a member of the clergy. But that individual cleric did nothing for some considerable time, for months – despite knowing by then that Whitsey had a record of paedophiliac behaviour.

I am lucky in that in some ways I have managed to separate 'the Church' from religion and my faith. I still have a strong faith, but I have very limited opportunities to share in collective worship or to talk about my faith – I am frightened of the Church and its latent power. Over the years since the abuse, I returned on occasion to the Church, and often found that its white maleness let me down. A big day for me and for my dad, by then happily married to the woman he left my mother for, was the day when Synod voted for women priests in 1987. We sat together and cried tears of joy. My tears were hopeful tears, tears expressing my happiness that the Church was fully inclusive at last. Of course those tears and that joy were premature.

We still have a broken Church, a Church where the moral compass seems to have gone awry, a Church where leaders are not prepared to accept liability and where survivors are treated with contempt. Safeguarding is not taken seriously. The Church does not even attempt to be self-policing. Even if it were to try, that is not the way forward; the Church and the behaviour of bishops, clerics and other individuals must be externally accountable. Instead, it is characterised by contradictions, self-aggrandisement, and by a lack of loving care.

After training as a tax inspector, **Dr Janet Lord** *moved into education and now works in a university in the North West of England. She is married with two daughters, and in her free time enjoys cookery, reading and choral singing.*

Chapter 22

Rape Followed by Bureaucracy

Matthew (as told to Linda Woodhead)

Matthew was 16 years of age when he was raped by a Church of England vicar in 1984. Because the vicar concerned committed suicide in June 2017, on the day he was due to appear in court, the media stories about the case always say that Matthew was 'allegedly raped'. This adds to his growing sense that he will never be taken seriously or see justice done.

I have got to know Matthew quite well in the course of interviewing him, and meeting him at various gatherings concerned with abuse in the Church of England. What follows is gathered from a number of interviews carried out in 2017–2018.

"You can use anything I've said," Matthew tells me at the end, "and everything I've shown you" (Matthew has let me look at any document I've asked to see in order to check the details of his story). "Nothing I write or say to you is confidential. It should all be in the open."

Matthew's rape

Matthew came from a broken home and the vicar, who lived alone in the vicarage, had taken him in:

"My mum was 17 when she had me. She was only married to my dad 11 months. One day [when Matthew, born in 1968, was 11 years old] she walked out of the house, leaving the front door open, and took a flight to Abu Dhabi and left me. My nan tried to look after me but couldn't cope, so she turned to the church for help.

"The first two nights with the vicar, he let me sleep in the spare room. I was still a kid, still riding my Chopper bike with my friends.

"The following night he told me to move into a bigger bedroom next to his. That night he came into my room: 'How are you? Are you settled?' He put his hand under the duvet and started playing with me. 'Don't you like that?' I said, 'no' and he left.

"The next night the same thing happened. And the next. Then he told me he had some other people coming to stay, so I had to share his room or I would have nowhere to go.

"When I was in his bed he turned me over and raped me. Then he went to sleep. I went to the bathroom. It was a mess with blood and everything. He really hurt me. He told me not to tell anyone. It went on for weeks.

"Then one day my nan came by. I thought I was in trouble. The vicar said, 'I need a word with your nan, go and sit in the kitchen.' Fifteen minutes later he came in: 'Your nan's gone.'

"The next day the bishop came. He spoke to the vicar, then to me. 'You can't stay here any longer,' he said. I said that I had nowhere to live, but that wasn't his problem. I presume the bishop knew because my Nan had contacted him, having got nowhere with my abuser.

"I got the bus to end of nan's road but I was too scared to go up the drive. I didn't know what they knew. I walked to Bradford and had two nights sleeping rough, then I found a bedsit to let. The landlord told me to go to and get housing benefit and supplementary assistance – I got an emergency Giro and moved into the grotty bedsit.

"Two days later there was a knock on the door and it was the vicar. He said he'd come to see how I was, and he didn't try anything on. The next day he came back with a two-ring table top cooker. That was the last time I ever saw him. I don't know how he knew where I was (maybe he had seen me and followed me); I don't know why he came. I didn't see my family for seven years.

"That summer of 1984 I took an overdose. After that I moved to a housing association flat and I got a job in hospitality, working for Trusthouse Forte. I have worked ever since. My dad found me after seven years, and it was brilliant, he was so kind to me. I have never made up with my mother. She drank a lot. I was ordained a priest in the Church of England in 2000 and my dad died in 1999, so he missed my ordination."

Matthew says he put the abuse to the back of his mind after that. It was only when a series of other events took place in 2012, involving possible harm to children in the school in his own parish, that it all came back. It was his struggle to get the problem taken seriously by his diocese of Sheffield that brought it back. That's when he says he disclosed his abuse, to his archdeacon, the suffragan bishop, and to the diocesan bishop and, in 2013, the police. He made a total of eight disclosures to church figures between July 2012 and June 2013.

"That's when my troubles really began. They all ignored me. In fact, my archdeacon took out a false disciplinary measure against me which was I think was to try and discredit me. No action was taken on this complaint, but I resigned from the Church. I couldn't go on. They did this, in my opinion, because I refused to be quiet about the reports of abuse of children in my parish and my own disclosures.

"I live alone now. I've never had a proper relationship. I've never had sex. I perceive it as dirty. I can appreciate companionship, I just avoid intimate relationships. I've coped by putting up a wall. I run my own business. I'm 50 years old. All I want is for it all to end so that I can get on with my life. Toby, my Yorkshire terrier, is my companion. He's also a victim of abuse! He was abused and as a result only got 2 teeth left and he's got a leg missing. He's 14 now." (Toby died shortly after the interview).

Matthew's Disclosures to Senior Clergy in the C of E

I ask Matthew what he feels about the vicar now, and I'm surprised by his response. The man killed himself in June 2017, on the eve of his criminal trial. He was facing six charges relating to sexual assaults – three counts of rape and three counts of indecent assault of a child. But Matthew speaks of him almost like a fellow victim.

He feels the vicar concerned was let down by an uncaring Church just as he has been: he was allowed to continue unchecked as a priest, then left without any support once the police investigation began (by which time he was retired and living in another diocese-but coincidentally with the same diocesan Matthew had disclosed to who had moved diocese). By then the vicar was known to be bipolar and had attempted suicide, and Matthew feels he should have been supported, whatever he had done. He was still a priest. Matthew wanted justice but feels that, as a priest with mental health problems the vicar should have received care from the church and then maybe he wouldn't have killed himself.

Now Matthew's anger is directed at the Church and the bishops as much as his rapist. "I told five senior clergy in all," he says, "and not one of them did a thing."

"Most of them say they have no recollection of the conversation. The diocesan bishop admits I disclosed to him verbally and twice in writing, but now says I implied that I didn't want him to take action. I didn't. Why would I do that? And the Archbishop I also wrote to just passed the buck back to the bishop and neither of them reported my disclosures to their safeguarding officer or the police. No one would lift a finger. I've had no apology, no nothing."

Because it involves disclosure to so many senior clergy, Matthew's case is incendiary. He acknowledges that sadly there is no law in the

UK that compels bishops or other senior officials to act on a disclosure of abuse, but he can't understand why they didn't want to take action or acknowledge his suffering. What hurts, he says, is the way he has been brushed off, dismissed, given no support. The more he asks for it, the worse it gets. He's trapped in a spiral, each party increasingly suspicious and angry with the other.

"It's worse than the abuse itself," he tells me. "I had faith in the Church, and all that has been taken away from me. Everything I built my life on, my vocation as well as my home and stipend and even my pension of course. It is cruel. Why won't they listen? Why won't they offer an apology? They won't even pay for my counselling. Why?"

The Clergy Discipline Measure

Having failed to get satisfactory personal or pastoral acknowledgement of his abuse, Matthew has tried using the only formal means available to him, the Clergy Discipline Measure. He has made complaints about the clergy he disclosed to, including the bishop, who is now in the same diocese as the retired abusive vicar went to live.

Matthew's first complaint about bishops not acting on his disclosures was submitted in 2016. The church refused to investigate them citing the church's own 'one-year rule', which says that complaints can only be brought within twelve months of the alleged offence being carried out. If it is longer than that – and it was in Matthew's case – then the people concerned are asked their opinion on the possibility of the one-year rule being extended. This meant that the church wrote to all the clergy concerned, including the abusing vicar. All of the clergy objected to an extension of the one-year rule. The vicar didn't reply (Matthew is particularly upset by this, by his alleged rapist being asked whether his complaint should be investigated – "they gave him more credence than me").

It is characteristic of cases in which people have been abused that it takes many years, often decades, before they are able to speak about what has happened to them. It's not clear why the senior clergy that Matthew complained about did not want an investigation to proceed, not least so that they could clear their names, but they did not. The President of Tribunals, who oversees the whole process, could have overturned their decision to dismiss the complaint, but ruled against it. His stated reason was that Matthew, having been subject to a CDM complaint himself, that he should have been aware of how the CDM worked, and that he should have brought his complaint earlier. "But

I had no idea," says Matthew. "Being the subject of a CDM (which was thrown out by the way) isn't the same as taking a case – it doesn't mean you know the rules. I certainly do now."

"I'm Tired and I Just Want it to Stop"

Matthew continues to battle for some resolution. He constantly asks himself whether he should just walk away. But the more he tries to get the Church to take his case seriously the more it resists, and the more he gets drawn in. His treatment means that his initial abuse can't start to heal, and he can't move on.

Even though Matthew has lost his faith, he is sanguine about the change: "I grew up with the church. My nan took me. I think I was like a lot of people who go to church totally oblivious to what goes on behind the scenes. 'Oh he's a lovely man, that bishop', and so on. It's done me good to stand back. I used to say mass from a book in front of me, but the more I examine what I once said and often taught by rote – 'a once for all and sufficient sacrifice' – the more I realise a lot of it was habit. Indoctrination almost. So maybe my abuse has been my saving.

"Hand-on-heart I don't know what effect the abuse has had on my life. I wonder sometimes. I wonder 'what if' it had never happened. I wonder if I would have had children. But I can't get it out of my head that sex is dirty. I can never go there."

At the time of writing Matthew is still pressing his case. He's got legal representation from the solicitor David Greenwood, and he's built an unexpected network of friends and supporters from those who have heard about his abuse, and in some cases been abused themselves. Recently another clergy woman, seeing his story in the media, got in touch to say she'd also been abused and disclosed to some of the same senior clergy and been dismissed in the same way.

So Matthew continues his struggle with more support than before. But he says repeatedly how tired he is. "I just want it to stop" is a constant refrain, but it will not stop. It is a case of an irresistible force (Matthew) meeting an immovable object (the upper echelons of the Church of England). Where the story will end no one knows.

"Are you a hero?" I ask Matthew, having heard his story of persistence. A true Englishman. "I'm no hero," he says, "just a 'common northerner' who can't abide injustice."

Matthew's account and story, as told to **Linda Woodhead.**

Chapter 23

Is 'Sorry' Really the Hardest Word?

Jayne Ozanne

Elton John's prophetic voice still rings true, to the Church at least: "Sorry seems to be the hardest word."

You will have heard many stories of abuse by now. Horrific stories – of sexual, emotional, physical and spiritual abuse. This book uncovers just the tip of an enormous iceberg. There are thousands more – each story uniquely different, about real people who have endured real pain.

Many of us have learned to carry the impact of what happened to us, to deal with it, to try to ensure that we are not crushed by it. Some of us have succeeded, some have not. Some of us have gone on to live relatively normal lives, some have not. Some have tried to shut out what happened, burying the trauma in the hope that it won't re-emerge – although sadly it nearly always does, often when we least expect it. Others carry the raw impact of their pain every day of their lives – open wounds that still fester and smart.

The important thing is that now, finally, some of our stories are coming out into the full light of day. No longer can the Church ignore or silence them. The Independent Inquiry on Child Sexual Abuse (IICSA) has managed to lift the lid on that. Others have been brought into public view by courageous survivors who have chosen to speak out in order to encourage others to do so. Some of these have even been bishops.

However, much abuse still sadly continues – often with the full knowledge and consent of the Church. I talk specifically about the issue of spiritual abuse, which is rife. It sadly affects many of our most vulnerable members: single mothers, divorcees, the disabled, and the LGBTI community. Indeed, all those who have been made to feel "less than" and are treated differently for who we are. Many of us are still treated as spiritual lepers by our churches. We are the untouchables, those who must have committed some unpardonable sin. Many of us have been told we need to be "transformed", that we need to repent of who we are or face Church discipline. Some of us have even been denied the sacraments. For us, scripture has been used as a weapon – to wound and curse, rather than to bring healing and hope.

It's appalling – the Church seems so adept at adding abuse on to yet more abuse, particularly in the way it has stood by when it has learnt of such practices and done nothing to intervene. Many of its leaders seem wedded to a Gospel of Law rather than to the Gospel of Love that our Saviour so powerfully taught and witnessed to us. They have forgotten that the Word of God is meant to bring life rather than to condemn, to save life rather than to destroy.

The one thing I have noticed as I have told my own story of abuse is that it has encouraged others to find their voice and tell me theirs. I get letters, emails, calls, tweets, direct messages, people waiting patiently to speak to me after I've preached – all wanting to share with me their story. They want to connect my pain to theirs – to say look, this has happened to me. It's a global community that needs to say #MeToo. Or, more specifically, #ChurchToo.

You see, people need to tell their stories, they need to be heard. It's a significant part of most people's healing. We need our pain to be recognised and understood, to be owned by someone in authority who can finally – often after several years – turn around and say to us something along the lines of:

I'm so very sorry, this was so very wrong. What happened to you should never have happened, you have been treated appallingly and I can't begin to understand the trauma that you've been through. Please try and forgive us for the pain that we, the Church, have caused you. You deserve far better, and we want to try somehow – with your help – to find a way to make amends.

My plea to Church leaders is: take the time to write in your own words, whatever they are. The key thing is that they need to come from your heart, and never from a prepared script. For only then can your words ring true, only then can they be heard as being meaningful and real. Heart needs to speak to heart – and when it does, it has the power to act as a salve, to be the balm of Gilead that the Psalmist tells us about in Psalm 79.

For only love can help heal these wounds, and that can never come from a formulaic liturgy or an off the peg letter sent out by an administrator on behalf of his or her boss.

No, the Church needs to do the hard graft of listening with open hearts and responding from the same. There is no short cut to saying sorry. It needs to be personal, human, and real: unique to each situation – just as each act of abuse was unique.

Abuse is an act perpetrated behind closed doors, hidden by shame for only a few to know about and see. Now it needs to be in the light of love and truth, with the fresh air of the Holy Spirit blowing through it.

But the problem, you ask, is who now can say 'sorry'? For it is never likely to be the person or persons who have perpetrated the abuse. Many are dead. Many are in denial. In fact, many are actually whole churches or movements that have still to recognise the trauma they have caused, believing that the "truth" they have meted out has "power to save", when in fact all it does in condemn, wound, and cause great mental anguish. It has led to parents disowning their children, friends turning their backs on their oldest mates, young people being abandoned at their point of greatest need – and countless, countless tears.

What is worse, the wounds are nearly always inflicted in the "name of love" by those we love – creating the gravest of wounds, rendering unsafe the one place we felt we belonged, and turning our safety net into a web that ensnares and entraps us.

Church leaders and churches are nearly always under authority. It is those in authority who need to own what has happened, even if it wasn't on their watch, and take full collective responsibility for what has happened in Christ's name.

So, Church, are you willing to take up the challenge? Have you the courage to listen to these testimonies? To make time to hear the heart-wrenching stories of individual and collective pain? The truth is that listening is crucifyingly difficult. Yet it is nothing compared to what we as individuals have had to go through – often alone, with little support or help. Surely, it's the least you can do in the circumstances?

The reality is, it seems, that many in authority are all too quick to want to jump this critical step. To run ahead and look at "good practice" of how the Church can make things better, do things differently, without understanding the bad practice that it has perpetrated and the lives that it has ruined. Not for many the hard and difficult work of owning and listening to the pain the Church has caused. Much easier to ignore it and just move on.

But history shows us that this is the worst possible route to take. Collective amnesia never works – the suppressed memories will haunt like a shadow, following the Church till it finally agrees to turn, face, and embrace its past. The memories need to be allowed to become part of it, and integral to what it must become: the Body of Christ.

The power of true penitence is arguably the most real and raw act that the Church can and should model. It is a central tenet of our faith.

It stems from a knowledge that all are broken and fallible human beings, each in need of forgiveness for the wrongs done – and often done in the name of Christ himself.

So how does the Church say sorry for the harm that has been done?

It starts with one important step. The step of courageously seeking truly to listen and learn.

Jayne Ozanne is a survivor of abuse, and a member of the Church of England's General Synod. She has previously been a member of the Archbishops' Council. She is founder and Director of the Ozanne Foundation.

Chapter 24

Power Abuse and the Bible: How Some Ministers Use Scripture to Control and Dominate Their Congregations

Stephen Parsons

The Gratification of Power as a Motive for Evil

When we review most forms of human evil we discover a common motive. Human beings sometimes do evil things to enjoy the gratification of exercising power. Behind such actions as robbery, sexual crime and even murder there is a desire by a perpetrator to be dominant or powerful in some way. Sadly, being a member of a religious group does not remove an individual from a propensity to seek and enjoy power. Some of these attempts are trivial and innocent, like the small boy wanting to be included in a church procession so that he can be the object of admiration. Power gratification is, more seriously, involved in actions that are outright evil – the grooming and sexual abuse of a victim. Power is not of course inevitably linked to gratification. Indeed, we speak of authority which is the legitimate exercise of the power that is needed in every institution. Somebody is appointed to take decisions and tell others what to do in an organisation, even the church. It is only when power becomes a craving that needs to be satisfied, that it is potentially a problem. When harm is caused to another person in exercising this kind of power, we rightly speak of power abuse.

In what follows I shall be exploring something about the nature of power in the church and the way that it is used abusively by some of its members. I will be focusing on one church culture, the conservative evangelical. In making the choice to focus mainly on this tradition, I am far from suggesting that church power abuse issues are unique to that culture. Indeed, in the Diocese of Chichester it was shown that Anglo-Catholic theological ideas around the practice of confession lay behind some of the abuses of power. I am in fact inviting church people from every type of background to examine their cultures and to be open to the way that power abuse can infect churches of any kind. The decision here to examine conservative teachings is a pragmatic one.

Conservative evangelical theology is well represented in Christian literature and thus fairly easy to study. It is thus a relatively straightforward matter to show how, in this tradition, some teachings do become corrupted and misappropriated by those who are seeking dominance and the enjoyment of power over others.

The Minister as a Focus of Power

In most congregations the clergy or ministers have a considerable amount of power. For some the level of status given to them by their position as a church leader is not enough. They feel it necessary to enhance further their power and influence. Conservative ministers typically do this by insisting on being the only voice heard from their pulpit. It is for them alone to interpret the 'inerrant' word of God. The role of being the sole interpreter of the words of God will quite quickly give to the minister an aura of quasi-divine power and authority.

Everyone would like to see ministerial power in a congregation being used creatively and well. The traditional Anglican approach to pastoral care is the attempt by the church leader to help people negotiate a path through the ambiguities and decisions of life in the best way possible. In this tradition it is understood as a kind of partnership between the cleric and the congregational member. In more conservative settings, where doctrine is taught without any sense of ambiguity or uncertainty, the style of pastoral support will often be quite different. Here we may find a relationship which is better described as being like master-servant or parent-child. It is no doubt the 'special' power given to 'inerrant' leaders that will affect the style and nature of the advice being offered. It comes to be far more like instruction and command. What is expected is obedience by the member of the congregation to the minister. He or she effectively speaks and acts with the authority of God.

In choosing three areas of church teaching where the Bible is sometimes used by a minister as a tool for exercising inappropriate power, I am far from claiming that these themes in any way exhaust the church's capacity to belittle individuals by the careful selection of texts from Scripture. I leave to one side the 'biblical' but questionable treatment and subordination of women, children and sexual minorities that these groups meet in many churches. The concern of this essay is to look at just some of the ways that a minister is able, according to whim, to use carefully selected texts to demonstrate and enforce his power in a congregation. By 'lording' it over others, the minister achieves the gratification of being important – a person of power and status. At the same time, he or she potentially becomes a danger to the well-being of those they serve.

The Bible Used to Bolster the Power of Christian Leaders

Twenty years ago, I was shocked and puzzled to hear a local Baptist minister preach on a New Testament verse, Hebrews 13.17, at a carol service when children were present. The verse contains the words "Obey your leaders and submit to them", but was wildly inappropriate to the occasion. I realised that this verse along with other scriptural quotations about obedience was of vital importance to this young minister. He looked after a small, financially struggling community and no doubt he felt this lack of professional and spiritual status keenly. Thus it was that the Hebrews passage and others emphasising the status of religious leaders appeared frequently in his sermons. Among these was the dubiously appropriate passage from Psalm 105.15 and 1 Chronicles 16.22: "Do not touch my anointed ones" (more often paraphrased as "touch not the Lord's anointed".)

The use of Bible passages which emphasise the need for obedience to a spiritual leader might just be an attempt to boost flagging morale in a pressured minister who has a tiny congregation. Equally and more dangerously it could be part of a wider power game to give total authority to an autocratic church leader who wants his own way in everything, spiritually and materially. Any demand for obedience can be the precursor to other kinds of power abuse. A child who has been encouraged to think of the minister or vicar as being the representative of God, is unlikely to have much in the way of self-protection if sexual favours are demanded. In short, demands for obedience backed up by quotations from scripture could mark the beginning of criminally abusive behaviour.

The use of texts to compel obedience to a minister is of course dangerous in further ways, not necessarily criminal. The leader may start to believe his own rhetoric that his words and thoughts are infallible and thus binding on all members of his congregation. We are here at the beginning of a full-blown narcissistic personality. The congregation becomes the emotional source to feed and gratify the minister's constant need for affirmation and high status. Congregation and minister in this way have become locked together in a circle of mutual need. This is unhealthy for all concerned. Unfortunately, the Bible provides further texts to consolidate the minister's control, should he choose to use them.

The Use of the Bible to Promote Belief in Demons

The second area where Bible texts are quoted as a means of enhancing the power of a minister is in the evoking of the demonic. When a confrontation takes place between an autocratic church leader and a questioning congregant, it can be presented as an example of satanic conflict. The narcissistic personality type referred to above, and which I believe to be common among church leaders, will find it difficult to tolerate any ambiguity or uncertainty. "He who is not with me is against me" (Matthew 12.30; Luke 11. 23) will often be heard in conservative congregations. The 'truth', which is always presented in black and white terms, will be as a light set over against the powers of opposition or darkness. Opposition to a leader is seen as darkness (the demonic) attacking the light.

The universe of the conservative Christian is also an environment fostering a great deal of fear. Any threat to a leader is met is met with the promise that any opposing group is on the way to eternal damnation and torment. In this fate they will be joined all who are not Christians or who go to churches not approved of by the preacher or leader. When church members fully internalise these terrifying threats, they can end up in a cycle of self-loathing and despair.

The key text that establishes the church and the world as being the platform for a constant cosmic battle between good and evil is Ephesians 6.12. Here the Christian is to see their role as that of a soldier fighting a battle against "the rulers, the authorities, against the cosmic powers of this present darkness, against the spiritual forces of evil in the heavenly places". This verse is frequently quoted to show Christianity as a struggle against supernatural evil. If the military metaphor of Ephesians 6 is overemphasised, we end up with something paranoid. The whole passage can also easily be read as a proposal for a Christian *Jihad*, one that may involve violence. The "powers of this dark world" could be any 'enemy' disliked by a leader. We are on the way to an atmosphere of intolerance and polarised thinking now so common in the States. Other scattered references to Satan and demons are found in the New Testament. These are preached about whenever the leader wants to raise the paranoid temperature within his congregation.

The Bible Used to Enable Ostracism and Shunning

The final method through which the Bible is used as a tool (or weapon) of power is in the way that it enables a Christian leader to expel followers who refuse to submit in obedience. We need briefly to ponder the devastating effect of an expulsion from a church congregation. A family may have spent decades in a congregation. Then, at the word of the minister, their membership is terminated. The sense of loss that can be experienced is like a bereavement. Social networks built up over a lifetime are sundered; the individual is cast out to a place of desolation and this is also a place considered to be on the way to hell.

The Christian leader who exercises the sanction of ostracising a congregational member will of course claim biblical authority for this action. He will refer to a passage such as Matthew 18:15–17. This appears to give a leader the authority to expel a 'brother' or 'sister' who has done something wrong. A similar power to root out a sinful member is implied in 1 Corinthians 5.5. "...[Y]ou are to hand this man over to Satan for the destruction of the flesh, so that his spirit may be saved in the day of the Lord." The issue of discipline within any congregation is of course sometimes going to be an extremely difficult area to manage. In some congregations, overseeing sexual abuse offenders who have spent time in prison is an issue.

Marriage failures within a congregation can also be very tricky situations to negotiate, particularly where both sides of a breakup are demanding pastoral support. It is not easy to avoid taking sides. Even more complicated is the situation is when two people become attracted to one another when one party is already married. Not everyone feels a sense of shame over an adulterous relationship. Applying Matthew's instructions to these complex scenarios is no straightforward matter.

This power to exclude and ostracise an individual within a church is something of great moment. As with any exercise of power, it can sometimes be used abusively. The threat to remove an individual or family is yet another tool of power able to boost the sense of control in a Christian leader. Even the thought of sanctions and exclusion can send a frisson of fear across a congregation. The raw power to shun and exclude does not have to be used very often for it to be a telling instrument of control. Such power, even as a threat, can discourage and demoralise a congregation.

One of the invidious aspects of a congregational expulsion is the way that an entire congregation may be drawn into the process. Each member individually has to join in. They are required to break off all contact with the victim(s) of exclusion. Even family bonds have to be broken. The reasoning is that the church in this way preserves its purity. A strong boundary is erected between the 'saved' and the damned.

This latter status would apply both to those who have been unwillingly expelled and those who have simply walked out. Of this latter group, one Christian leader (not Anglican) used to quote 1 John 2.19: "They went out from us, but they did not belong to us." The frequent quoting of this verse conditioned the congregation to believe that anyone who left that church for whatever reason was on their way to a state of damnation. Everyone had a duty to shun such people as well as collude with lies that were told about them. Children also were caught up in these dynamics of exclusion. The pain on all sides was massive.

Conclusions

We have outlined three distinct ways that the Bible is sometimes harnessed to gain enhanced power for a Church leader. We have suggested that when the Bible is used in this way it effectively can become a tool of abuse for this leader. The examples we have given all illustrate harmful behaviour within churches which do not involve sexual abuse. Autocratic church power will often manage to wound and damage the victims. The Church needs to have a far better understanding of the dynamics of power and its abuse as well as understand how this whole area is of major importance for all churches. A style of bible teaching found across many conservative inerrantist churches, is, we would claim, an important contributor to these kinds of abuses.

Much more work needs to be done to challenge such abusive use of Scripture. Cruel and vindictive behaviour towards individuals, even when it is not technically criminal, has no place in our churches. It is quite simply bullying and abuse. The ability to quote texts from Scripture to back up this form of behaviour will never justify or condone it. It must be outlawed in the name of the one who taught us not to dominate or to 'rule' but rather be the "the willing servant of all".

Stephen Parsons is a retired Anglican priest who lives in the Diocese of Carlisle. He has studied the issue of church abuse since the mid-90s and edits a blog, www.survivivgchurch.org.

Chapter 25

Sundered Bodies and Broken Hearts: A Eucharist of Rebirth?

Carrie Pemberton Ford

A Fugue

We are in the midst of a fugue. The opening chords were heard two millennia ago when Mary was informed by Gabrielle that she would become pregnant, or was it suppressed laughter at the entrance of Sarah's tent, as two visitors talked with her octogenarian husband about her up–coming pregnancy? A son who would birth a nation, immense and incalculable, like the grains of sand which surrounded them. Was it the percussion of wings in Nazareth, or was it in the soft tones of a man speaking to a grieving woman, in the early morning in a garden outside the Damascus Gate in Jerusalem, hard by the favoured location for the Roman state to crucify enemies of the state, and those designated for death by the Jewish religious authorities.

On reflection the first breath, the raising of the baton was at the inception of the world, as the ice mass formed and gases exploded across the universe. A single voice spoke, some say it rumbled, "Let there be light." No matter. Voices have made their entrance and the fugue has been taken up by others, building in its complexity across time and space. One part successively taken up and refreshed by others, building its rich texture through interweaving, augmentation, reversals, interjections, contrapuntally building across the episodes through time the central subjects. Light out of darkness, Life through death, Love over hate – the signature tune of *Logos*.

Sundered Bodies

Christianity was birthed in sundered bodies. This volume is full of accounts of broken-ness. Of lives wrenched out of shape, disfigured, surrendered to the full force of public shame. It is one of the voices which is always present in the fugue as it moves across the years, decades, centuries, playing out the counter-subject of Light first announced in the heart of the cosmos.

Mary's body, like the two thousand women who will have given birth by the time you have read this essay, will physically have experienced a sundering so profound, that none of them will have again precisely the same bodily relationship with the world in which they conceived. Labour can leave a woman utterly exhausted, retching, screaming with the pain of third stage contractions, partly immobilised if epidurals are deployed, terrified, exhilarated, accompanied, alone, euphoric with Etonox or birthing hormones, facing death, appalled, cut open, up-ended, humiliated, holding onto her own umbilical cord with life, co-creator and devastated Eve. Some 303,000 women a year die in childbirth, or as a result of complications arising from pregnancy. This equates to about 830 women dying each day. Four women will have died from pregnancy or childbirth-related complications as you read through this essay. Mary came out of the ordeal alive, as did the infant Jesus.

As Bishop Jeffrey John reflects in his foreword to *Living the Magnificat – Affirming Catholicism in a Broken World*, God in the person of Jesus "becomes utterly powerless; totally at the mercy of his mother and he shares all the risks of a first century pregnancy". The incarnation project is attached to the destiny of Mary's placental health, as the Christ child grows in her womb. God is "totally powerless: God himself is dethroned". A message which churches over-bloated with ideologies of Lordship, Prince Bishops, the mediation of power, and *ex-cathedra* expulsions could do well to consider.

Stepping Over the Bodies

For most Anglicans reading this essay, your experience of attending church at Easter, or Christmas, or maybe for a wedding, or indeed baptism, or as a regular attender of your local church, has been to pass through grounds, step over thresholds, where hundreds of bodies lie undisturbed beneath the soil. In caskets if cremated, in various styles of carbon archives, some simply wrapped in muslin sheets, these bodies have been buried in haste after the crises of plague, or in the full decorum of an appropriately curated funeral, with the intervention of professional mortician, with song, with speeches, with poems, with tears, with the full craft of human artistry to create a social container through which the brokenness of death can be negotiated, and life continue. Light.

However sometimes as the eulogies are prepared, prayers said, family and friends gather to say goodbye, the one in the casket is not the only one who is lying supine. A Facebook support group, constituted by dozens of those who have experienced over the last decades the rupture of promises made by their clergy spouses, and the demolition of their past 'joint' identity, vocation, and current safety shattered in various painful ways, is populated with painful accounts of the trauma of dealing with the 'lies' which cover over what are frequently referred to as 'clergy misdemeanours'. The more personal the abuse, the more difficult the recovery.

> It was like it wasn't Stephen[1] they were burying. I wanted to stand up and shout out – "he betrayed me, he betrayed all of you, he betrayed his children, he betrayed God." I wanted to scream " I hate him, and I loved him. I stayed with him and I should have left. He lied, betrayed, punched and broke me, please let me bury that man, that broken betrayal of a man. I need to bury Stephen not an Icon.

> I needed to bury him, my marriage and all of his broken promises. I needed the support of my friends and the congregation to do that, to bury him truthfully. A priest to help do that to acknowledge the nightmare I am living through – and I couldn't find it. None of it.

A Eucharist of Broken Hearts and Death

Now the voice of the Eucharist enters. Sublime, ethereal. Yes, contested over time with whole nations divided, and thousands of lives incarcerated under the trope of transubstantiation and the severance of this meal from the word of God, light and dark, life and death. The Eucharist in which the Church from the earliest remembrance of Christ's journey towards betrayal, abandonment, and death, captures in the narrative of Jesus' last supper a cup of wine, and unleavened bread broken. The light and life of resurrection hope, of a body re-membered in this repetition of his final meal.

My former professor at Cambridge, David Ford, described the Eucharist being the place where we are "face to face (in faith and hope) with the one who commands that this be done in memory of him – the baptised self in the routine of being fed and blessed". As Karen O Donnell remarks in her paradigm-shifting work, *Broken Bodies*, the Eucharist for Ford "creates an expectation of death in its focus on the Last Supper and thus in this non-identical", but transferred repetition into our landscape of desire and hope, "celebrates the death of Christ until he comes". Ford had his first experience of death early, close up, personal, as someone whose own father died as Ford entered puberty,. That loss, rupture and devastation healed in the 'Tragedy and

---

1 From a conversation in 2018. Name altered to protect the source.

Atonement' being played out in the cosmos, rehearsed through the liturgy of the Church which has recently been reconsidered by Karen O'Donnell in her recent book *Broken Bodies: The Eucharist, Mary, and the Body in Trauma Theology.*

A Crucified God

Crucifixion and the broken body of Christ, is one of the central narratives of the Church and the Gospels which form the core of the New Testament Scriptures. Crucifixion before resurrection. A body nailed up on a cross, slowly asphyxiated by the weight of his own body.

In the years after the devastation of the second world war there was a revelation of Germany's and her Axis allies' commitment to the destruction of millions of European Jews; hundreds of thousands of Roma and Slavs; thousands of those with disabilities; those of different ethnicities; those unnumbered gay, lesbian, trans people who were categorised as "Untermenschen" ("subhumans" in English). For the German Reformed theologian Moltmann it was this which severed the twentieth century's artery of a God who could cede place to late enlightenment, secularised humanity.

In his two defining works, *A Crucified God* and *A Theology of Hope*, Jurgen Moltmann, writing in the 1970s, described a God who is alongside humanity in its suffering, who is caught up in the deep suffering which humanity experiences: in the extermination camps which rot in the fields of contemporary Poland, in the horrors of warfare, in the desperation of those who feel that God has abandoned them. His presence is in that very moment of abandonment. There is no place where God is not present. Moltmann's God is not distant, aloof, unmoved, unempathetic. Moltmann's God picks up the theme of John Robinson's *Honest to God* – a God who not only hears the cries of those who are suffering, but is with them, viscerally, in their embodied experience of suffering and expulsion.

The Cheerful Hymn, by Lucy Berry

Sex, drugs, excessive rock-and-roll
Were kept at bay. They passed us by.
We have declined to be involved
In that which caused our Christ, to die.
Before this church dies on its feet
Christ, give them something dark to eat.

Our hands are clean. We like and greet
Each other in a cheerful way.
We let no pain contaminate
Our cleanly, sacred, Sabbath day.
Before this church dies on its feet
Christ, give them something dark to eat.

We leave despair outside the gate
As we have done these hundred years.
Our church has never been a place
For Life and Death and hopes and fears.
Before this church dies on its feet
Christ, give them something dark to eat.

Vile parents, violence, abuse;
Our church was never home to these.
No seething misery or hate,
No personal Gethsemanes.
Before this church dies on its feet
Christ, give them something dark to eat.

We never brought our suicides
Or failed loves, or lost pregnancies
For people who are really good
Are not dealt troubles such as these.
Before this church dies on its feet
Christ, give them something dark to eat.

So, on the surface, let us move,
Un-agonised, towards our heaven
Keen not to feel the slightest thing
For which we might not be forgiven.
Before this church dies on its feet
Christ, give them something dark to eat.

© Kevin Mayhew

Reaching into the Fugue we find another sign within the Eucharist, with potential power for reconstituting our failures in 'fessing up', in nurturing fledgling movements of life, of taking the full horrors of life, within and without church, from the bread ripped open, and the wine poured to revive us in the very presence of death.

A Nursing Mother

Just as the horror of genocide forced one of the twentieth century's most influential Protestant theologians to return to the central moment of the sundered body on the cross: so has the emergence of women's gendered experiences of rape within the context of civil and international warfare, harassment and abuse in the public and private sphere; grief; desolation; and mobilisation against the forces of corrupted regimes, drug cartels and dictatorships in Latin America forced through a fresh exploration by liberation, queer and feminist theologians of what is being captured in the Eucharist. Which event are we celebrating? Is Christianity a 'cult of death', an empathy-enriching rehearsal of a singular tragedy of a young revolutionary who was raised into a God, or are there strands of the Fugue which have been left behind in our shared but buried history?

Under the noise of death, and suffering, the fanfare trumpets of resurrection, is there is another voice to be heard?

A Holistic Eucharist?

What if the Eucharist is about the whole of life? Not just the focus of death, sympathy, mortification and hope of resurrection; but the incarnation, nurturance, failures, confusions, accidents and contingencies alongside the western epicentre of betrayal, crucifixion, resurrection and reception of the Spirit? What if the baby surrendered to the fierce fragility of a young woman's womb, sundering her body, birthed in blood, urine and amniotic fluid, nurtured from the breast of Mary, is also the one who nurtures us in this archetypal feast for the community of faith? What if the blood, urine and amniotic fluid come all together? That there is no birth without this. No possibility of life without this chaos, this mess of bodily and social reproduction? Not as an excuse to be pissed on from on high. But that the blood of life, the heartbeat of the universe comes mixed in this way and the body of the Church must ingest, digest, process it all.

Paul Bradshaw and Maxwell Johnson in their work on the Eucharistic liturgies assert that strands in early Christian practice "viewed the eucharistic elements as life-giving and spiritually nourishing rather than in sacrificial terms". Further, that early Christians sought to view the "primary ritual of intimacy with the Divine not in terms of the horror and violence of the cross, but rather with the miracle of the Annunciation-Incarnation event with all its generative and life giving promise".

Brothers and Sisters with Christ

Clement of Alexandria used the imagery of breast milk and drew the symbolism across from the nourishment received in spiritual teaching of believers, with the 'drinking the Word of God who is the milk' which has been recently asserted by Karen O'Donnell as referring to a Eucharistic practice of not only drinking wine at the Eucharist, but also on occasion liturgically partaking of a milk and honey cup attested to in the third century text *The Apostolic Traditions.*

Fascinatingly, O'Donnell points to the fact that those who drank from the same wet nurse within the clan, regardless of their actual genetic background, were seen in ancient cultures as milk siblings. O'Donnell points out that this brother and sister milk sibling language, was entirely appropriate to the familial setting in which the early Church functioned. Furthermore, breast milk conferred 'not only kinship but also the characteristics of the mother' – through the milk which she bestowed. By inference then a eucharistic cup which is drunk as 'full of the milk provided through the flesh of Jesus is to consume milk that is full of the essential characteristics of Christ'.

Whether feeding from the breasts of Christ, or remembering the God Bearer who fed the infant Christ with milk endowed by the birthing of the Christ child, the third Century *Odes of Solomon* see disruptive gender images in play:

A cup of milk was offered to me
And I drank it with the sweetness of the Lord's kindness
The Son is the cup
And he who was milked, the Father,
and (the one) who milked him, the Spirit of holiness
Because his breasts were full
And it was not desirable that his milk should be poured
out/discharged for no reason/uselessly'

The Fugue Augmented / or the Fugal State

Our fugue moves into its final augmentation as we reflect on what is brought to the wider chorus of voices assembled here in this volume as we explore a deeper and more holistic Eucharistic theology in our consideration of what it means to be Church today in all our disrupted, avoidant, disrespected, battered, betrayed, side-stepping, denial-ridden, harassing, judgemental, opinionated, compromised, protectionist, cloven-tongued, and avoidant behaviours. Read any of the contributions in this anthology of fracture, and out calls a voice of a betrayed spouse, a raped child, a bullied employee, a groomed sexually abused teenager, a neglected widow, a contemporary *Untermenschen* – a sub-human by virtue of sexuality, gender, ethnicity, dis/ability, her/ his story.

One of the key ideas which has accompanied my vocation and work in counter trafficking, supporting victims of all sorts of gender based violence and criminality over the years, has been the centrality of the victim's voice, his/her narrative and the ground rules of validation, attention to feelings, hearing out their story, affirming their integrity, placing their journey into context and the questions raised by their voice, front and central. It is what we do every time we settle to listen to the accounts of the Gospels and attend to the parables, teachings and stories of Jesus of Nazareth as he and his community found them-selves inexorably caught in the playing out of the Passover tragedy; betrayal, grief, death and 'on the run' refugees hunted down by the State as part of a putative Messianic revolution. Except we forget that this story, this theme of hymnody and creed, is a narrative of victims, of those who suffered deeply for the 'faith that was inside them', because this narrative has been in the hands of the victors and the power elite for over fifteen hundred years.

And so to the Church and many of those lulled into a sense of false entitlement in the Church community. We have, I venture, entered into a Fugal state. Not the musical theme, but the Fugal state also known as a dissociative fugue. Here an individual is in:

> a psychological state in which a person loses awareness of their identity or other important autobiographical information and also engages in some form of unexpected travel. People who experience a dissociative fugue may sudden-ly find themselves in a place, such as the beach or at work, with no memory of how they got there. Similarly, they may find themselves somewhere in their home, such as a closet or in the corner of a room, with no memory of going there. The DSM-5 refers to dissociative fugue as a state of "bewildered wan-dering".

Is this where we have gone as a Church – where we have lost our iden-tity and as followers of the *way*, lost our sense of purpose, and our deep sibling identity with the narrative of Christ?

The Eucharist of Rebirth – Recovering a Lost Identity

Reconnecting with these other voices in the Fugue of the Logos, the initiating rumble at the core of our universe, and the heart of our faith, offers a theme of recovery for a Church which is broken, and lives which are lying sundered outside the threshold of organised religion and Church. Lives where many feel the cruel asphyxiation of crucifixion, being hung out and abandoned by the 'party' which is going on inside the gates of their 'new Jerusalem'.

What about all the places and relationships which are broken, destroyed, rotting? All the graves where sundered bodies are dug in by the institution, or by those 'in control'? These are shallow graves of convenience, done on the fly, and the power of generation forces pieces of these broken bodies up through the soil. All the voices brought into the fugue need their place to speak. Without them the fugue itself collapses, loses its vitality and structure.

As a Church we are used to the motif of suffering. It is not only locked into four centuries of church practice across the years of European Inquisition, burnings, excommunication, expulsions and incarcerations as the processes of the Enlightenment swept across Europe and confronted a Church State alignment which enforced old riffs, refusing the change in rhythm sounding through the breakthroughs of contemporary science, the emergent sympathies of a liberal humanism and the deconstruction of old hierarchies of knowledge and the Divine Right of Kings.

We have validated suffering. Not only in the blood of martyrs which is relentlessly spilt in every generation. We are used to the notes of crucifixion – depending on where we are set, this varies in its 'lively sense'. Those having suffered the cruelty of Soviet repression of both Orthodox and Protestant Churches in the last century, can join with those in Egypt, China, Nigeria, Uganda, Sudan, Brazil, Syria, and testify to its present reality as part of our condition as those who hold to 'another way'.

But in 'validating' suffering, internalising the condition as the very stuff of discipleship, disciples can be rendered passive in the face of suffering, their own as well as others', rather than vomiting up the poisonous food of hierarchical insouciance; exclusionary behaviours; jealousies; ego-led jockeying for positions; phobias of all sorts pertaining to sex, class, ethnicity, sexuality, physical abilities, gender. Whited Sepulchres. Many of those writing in this collection will have had invoked by others usually dressed in various shades of purple or black, the 'suffering of Christ' to validate negligence, organisational passive brutality, exclusion of their gifts, silencing of their unique, irreplaceable voice in the great choral work of the Logos which is being sung across the generations, races, and time.

Critical to surviving a Fugal state, is to bring the sufferer to a place where they can announce their narrative and express their desires for restitution, justice, freedom from a place of safety. This is the journey from victimhood to emerging as a survivor and one who will eventually flourish. It requires all the resilience which we carry within ourselves to survive, and depends in significant part to having radically safe places of support, welcome, non-judgement, openness, reception, to heal traumatised memory, and restitch the basic fabric of life back together with 'siblings' accompanying and yes, at times, carrying us along the way. As even in his transition from death to life, Jesus is supported by Nicodemus, received by Mary, anointed by Mary Magdalene, in Michelangelo's Florenza Pieta. Survival is a communal task. It is the new communion, displaying that we are children of God, milk siblings, who love and practically care for one another, nurtured at a common breast, to reveal God's purposes of justice, love, mercy for the whole of creation.

All who hear the strains of the *Logos*, to "come unto me", who have witnessed the "overshadowing of the power of the Most High'", who have responded to the invitation to "come and dine with me", are called to partake in the great Eucharist of thanksgiving and nourishment. The Eucharistic meal is then about the whole of life – the incarnation, nurturance, feeding from the breast of Christ, the compassion of Mary, the generosity of Joseph, the fierce obedience of Jesus with a new voice on the legal codes and restrictions of the Levitical code, re-situating clean and unclean from the physical into the alignment of the heart, welcoming all the excluded ones, Samaritans, migrants, prostituted, silenced and blinded, socially or physically deemed as contaminated, imprisoned, all the queer ones, to a radical community fellowshipping in equality. Their mandate is to love one another in the way in which the *Logos* loves. And where that love has been defaced, abused, ruptured, betrayed; to call out the truth, for healing, for justice, for renewed life.

Our broken Church, and all broken communities, are called to this promise for healing, which is the second great fugue of creation. As milk siblings, all who have eaten this bread, and drunk the milk and honey of Christ's life from a common cup are equal in the community of faith. The challenge for us reaching into the twenty first century is, how to resist the temptation of virtual fratricide, genocide, and femicide which offers itself as the easy solution to the guilt, shame, fear, anxiety, ignorance, club comfort which keeps us separated from one another. Destruction of the other is no longer an option. We have put away the burnings and the stake. We should not walk away from milk siblings. We share a common breast. We wake up our Church from its Fugual State, its amnesia, and remember our true vocation.

The fugue continues. The first voice waits to be taken forward in a myriad different variations within the great chorus. Are our hierarchies ready to practice the skills required to sing it, and open up the fugue for its next progression to the voices waiting to join their part within the 'church choir'? – else the part will move across to others whose voices are ready to sing the healing of the nations which the voice of Magnificat proposed. Listening attentively to the parts being offered here in this collection may be disorientating particularly for those in roles of authority, and difficult at first to incorporate into the repertoire which has been inherited. But this is the gift of fugue. Dissonance, contrapuntal disruption, opens up the piece for greater exploration of the initiating theme which was sounded as the baton was raised. Let there be Light. We awaken.

Rev Dr Carrie Pemberton Ford, author, speaker, academic and priest, is the Executive Director for CCARHT, a counter human trafficking think tank, based in Cambridge, working inter-disciplinarily across the University. www.ccarht.org. She was the first ordained clergywoman to be appointed to Government Office as a Woman's National Commissioner in 2004, and was a founder member of the National Executive of WATCH Women and the Church.

Chapter 26

Church, Cricket, Elephants and Armies

Martyn Percy

This piece was written after the Independent Inquiry into Child Sexual Abuse (IICSA) hearings into the Diocese of Chichester, in March 2018.

> The Church of England... [has] an understated ecclesiology coupled to a re-served English manner that makes for a nation – or at least a national church – that is, well, just too polite, settled and civilised to get very enthusiastic about anything. As one commentator has recently noted, can it really be any accident that cricket is the preferred game of the clergy in the Church of England? An individual, yet collaborative game; full of manners, codes of conduct – 'sport-ing' sport; strenuous and restful by turns, combining subtlety and strength (speed is rarely valued); where all may have different gifts and functions, yet be equally valued; and where the side about to lose can gain an honourable or even heroic draw, either due to rain or bad light. Results really don't matter; it's how you play the game.
>
> Martyn Percy, *Thirty-Nine New Articles: An Anglican Landscape of Faith,* (Canterbury Press, 2013, page 157)

In David Tracy's *The Analogical Imagination* (SCM Press, 1981) the au-thor invites us to think of analogical and other ways of viewing the life of faith, rather than just through the lens of doctrine or tradition. So just for the moment, we are going to think of the current ecclesial crisis in the Church of England as something like a cricket Test Match. Please bear with me as I explain.

I have been watching something like a long game of cricket over the past three weeks. I refer to the Test Match that is IICSA – the Independent Inquiry into Child Sexual Abuse – that has been looking into the Church of England's record on safeguarding. IICSA works with case studies, and the Church of England found itself fielding a side that mainly consisted of players drafted in from the Diocese of Chichester, with a smattering of others representing the National Safeguarding Team, the House of Bishops, and other bodies within the church.

This particular IICSA process has, after all, been something of a spectator sport. The inquiry has been live-streamed, and open to the public. The Church of England has batted and bowled. It has faced an arsenal of bowling: bouncers, googlies, daisy-cutters, and spin; medium and fast-paced bowlers. There have been, for bishops and officers of the church, lengthy stints at the crease, facing these bowlers. We have watched as the interrogators have batted too. Mostly, they have taken safe singles. There have been very few big sixes or grand fours. They take a few runs here, and a few there. But over after over, the score has piled up. Like snowflakes on a flat roof, the weight has told.

The batting from the Church of England has been pretty awful. One bishop – out for a duck on virtually every ball he faced – blamed his team-mates, or his kit, or his secretary. Another bishop seemed to think he should not need to bat. Other officers and officials representing the church blamed their colleagues. Time after time, witnesses for the Church of England were caught, bowled out, leg-before-wicket, or just run out. Indeed, there was something of a running theme throughout the three weeks.

The Church of England is not really a team at all. It is just a rather motley collection of individuals who are vaguely relating to one another. There was no joined-up strategy. There was no game plan. But no one is prepared to accept responsibility for the fact that after three weeks, the Church of England had scored nothing. There were no points on the board.

In contrast, IICSA, simply by sticking to their game plan, amassed a massive total, and eventually declared. The Church of England, who had pinned its hopes on rain stopping play so it could claim a draw, went home utterly defeated. As a spectacle – and in terms of professionalism, accountability and integrity – I can only say it was like watching Australia taking on a scratch second eleven from a local pub that had met in the bar a few hours earlier. They had drunk a few pints, and fancied their chances. But you just felt embarrassed for the Church of England; for their hubris, folly and misplaced self-regard. This Test Match was a humiliation and annihilation for the church; excruciating viewing, frankly.

The media barely covered this debacle, I suspect, because the three weeks have amounted to something of a slow death for the Church of England as an operational public body. In effect, IICSA offered us a ringside seat to watch a whole elephant being eaten. Slowly, mouthful by mouthful. But that is what IICSA did. Not so much eating the Church of England for breakfast, as in fact consuming the body over the course of several weeks.

As Peter Drucker said, "culture eats strategy for breakfast". And, whatever defence strategy the Church of England might have had for engaging in the process of defending its practice and reputation in safeguarding, the legal culture that IICSA embodies just ate the Church of England up ... bit by bit. In fact, so slow was this at times, I am not sure the officers defending the Church of England even saw or realised it was being consumed, so absorbed were their advocates in their own bubble of self-justifying rhetoric. At the risk of mixing metaphors, the IICSA cross-examiners were first-class. The Church of England, in contrast, revealed itself to be wholly amateur. Not even well-meaning amateurs, alas, as time and again the reputation of the Church of England was placed at a premium, and well above the needs or interests of those who had been abused.

To paraphrase (and slightly twist) the words of Winston Churchill: never, in the field of ecclesial conflict, has so much been owed, by so few, to so many. The Church of England revealed itself to be a delinquent polity – a culture where minor oversights, dubious legal shortcuts, file-shredding or record burning, forgetfulness, errors, incompetence and culpability were routine, and added up to one thing. Here is a body you cannot trust. You should not even try to trust it. You should not make the mistake of placing your life and safety in the hands of people who would so lightly squander your interests, and who then go on to wash their hands of responsibility in public.

In their intriguing book *Mistakes were made – but not by me* (Houghton Mifflin Harcourt, 2017), Carol Tavris and Elliot Aronson explain how it is that the individuals and institutions which make catastrophic errors that cause damage and pain to others, or simply mistreat them, can live with themselves and justify their actions or inaction. The key to this, Tavris and Aronson argue, is that the individuals or institutions responsible for the neglect or abuse are able to calm their cognitive dissonance by creating fictions that absolve themselves of responsibility. Thus, the belief that we are clever, moral and right masks behaviours that are idiotic, immoral and wrong.

This helps to explain why a bishop in the Diocese of Chichester can just deal with the history of abuse in his patch – happening under his watch, and right under his nose – with little more than a shrug of the shoulders. It wasn't his fault. He was only obeying orders. Responsibility lies further up the chain of command. He's just the bishop of an area in a Diocese.

It all feels a little bit like the cognitive dissonance of the neighbourly residents living close to those concentration camps in the Second World War. They had often been the direct beneficiaries of the cheap or free labour in their own gardens, factories or businesses, but they had never sought to ask about the turnover of labour:

> Where was that nice young hard-working Polish Jew who worked on the factory floor for us last week? He mopped the floor superbly: morning, noon and night... almost as though his life depended on it. Not available now, huh? Ah well, no matter – but you say there are a couple of new Hungarian Jews I can have, and who work just as hard? Thank you. I don't know where your camps get this free labour supply from, but it is impressive. The war must be going well for us. Oh, by the way, can you do something about the smell from those incinerators? It can be awful when the wind blows over the town, what with the smoke and the ashes. Yes, I know you are just burning old clothes and rubbish to keep the camps pristine and free from diseases. I do appreciate that. Well done. Keep up the good work.

This may seem unfair to the Church of England at IICSA. But too many times, we heard church leaders utter phrases akin to, "I was just obeying orders", "it was not my responsibility to report this," or "I had no idea this was going on" – and more besides. Archbishops passed blame on to their bishops. The bishops passed the blame on to their staff. The National Safeguarding Team (NST) seems to have been blamed by everyone. But the NST appeared to respond to this by referring the blame back up the chain of command. Everyone passed the buck. Everyone knew a little, but no one chose to know enough. It seems that the cultures of abuse were ultimately no one's fault. So no one did anything. Everyone else was to blame.

Cognitive dissonance and wilful blindness plays a part in the institutional behaviour patterns we have seen in the Church of England, as disclosed by IICSA. But can the Church of England really see what has become of itself? I think it can't. As Lord Molson once remarked, "I will look at any additional evidence to confirm the opinion to which I have already come."

And what is that opinion, exactly? The Church of England likes – perhaps loves – itself. It cannot understand why it is even at the batting crease, facing all these awkward balls from IICSA, over after over. It should just be allowed to get on with itself – immune from public inquiry and those tiresome worldly professional standards.

It was Iris Murdoch who said, "Love... is the extremely difficult realisation that something other than oneself is real."

But if you only love yourself, the only real thing that matters is the real you. This helps explain why the National Safeguarding Team can't even manage some simple arithmetic. Because the people – the victims here – literally don't count.

At General Synod in February 2018, when a Synod member asked the Bishop in charge of Church of England's Safeguarding how many open cases of safeguarding the Church was currently dealing with, he didn't know. The best he could do was to say that there had been "around 3,300" safeguarding concerns or allegations last time they had looked, which was in 2016. This figure was subsequently adjusted, corrected, and further qualified.

The honest answer is that the Church of England seems not to really know. Numbers are rounded off to the nearest hundred. Victims, it seems, are like statistical casualties recorded in an epic battle of yore. They are numbers; not real people in their own here and now, trying to piece together their shattered lives. The tragedy – and indeed farce – of the Church of England's performance at IICSA, is that it came across, consistently, as quite clueless.

Like many loyal servants of the Church of England, I have watched IICSA over the past three weeks with a growing, troubling, deep sense of shame. This is a hard thing to admit. To know that you belong to a body where you can no longer believe or trust the account of the polity and practice that is being offered in defence of its behaviours by its own leaders. To know that the real victims in this tragic farce who are still waiting for basic, fundamental rights that should be givens for the church – recognition, remorse, repentance – are abused twice over.

In the first instance, it is by their actual abuser. The second time, and far worse, is the subsequent abuse perpetrated by the Church. For this is a church that is deaf, dumb and blind – and seemingly wilfully indifferent to the suffering undergone by those abused – and then addresses this with little more than an incompetent veneer of safeguarding practice, which only further compounds the original act of abuse.

In all this, the Diocese of Chichester stands as the 'exemplar' of the Church of England. Herein, arguably, we catch a glimpse of the biggest risk that now faces the institution. So let us return, once again, to the analogical imagination. The Church of England is not like the Bank of England. The latter is a body, that when the Governor speaks and announces a rise or drop in interest rates, or some other fiscal policy or measure, that is what the Bank of England does. It has clear policies and practices. It speaks as a corporate and united entity; a single body.

The Church of England, in contrast, is nothing of the sort. But if the Church of England is not like the Bank of England, to what shall we compare it? It's more like the British Army, to be frank. Who runs the British Army? Well, they are Her Majesty's armed forces, but it has been some while since the crowned head of the nation spearheaded any actual attack on the enemy.

The Secretary of State for Defence is more usually found behind her or his desk than at the front of an assault on an enemy line. The generals might lead an attack – but from where is this led, exactly? They don't usually lead from the front, as they are more often in an 'operations room', sometimes not even in the same country as the military action.

When it comes to asking what the British Army is, well, it depends whom you ask. Is it the Defence Contract Procurement Department who buy the bullets? Or is it the soldiers who shoot them? Is it the Army Medical Corps? Or is it the artillery? Or the Cavalry – and if by Cavalry, do you mean people in tanks, or trotting along on horses for the Trooping of the Colour? If you want to be defended, are the Marines the best? Or the Highland Regiment? Or the SAS?

Who speaks for the British Army? It could be a retired general. It could be a serving one. Or it could be Colonel Blimp next door, who last saw action in Aden, or had a father who fought against the 'fuzzy-wuzzy' insurgents. It could be almost anyone connected with the Army. Anyone.

The Church of England has the same kind of problem managing its identity and issues. Who speaks for the Church of England on women bishops, or on same-sex marriage? The bishops? Yes, to a point. But also clergy, laity, synod members, retired vicars and others. Lambeth Palace may field a 'spokesperson for the Church of England'. But they don't usually speak for me, I tend to find. Every time they do speak, of course, they send an implicit message – wholly unintended.

Whisper it: 'We are small'. If someone can speak for all of us, we are the few, not the many. In becoming manageable, we become comprehensible, and in the course of that single move, the Church of England becomes a different animal in public discourse: a subject that is easy to grasp, so can also be easily discarded and dismissed.

Of course, I do understand the motivations and desire to have all the bishops 'on message'. But getting them all 'on the same page' only pasteurises the plurality of the Church of England, and turns it into one homogenous gloop. The instinct of a corporate boss is to shape and control. But the trouble is that a leader good at corporate-speak and practice will reduce the size of body to something he or she can manage. Enforced 'corporate-speak' shrinks the Church; it reduces its breadth. It is just like someone speaking for the British Army – unconsciously, you know this should not really be possible. More deeply, you know that if it is possible, it must be a very small armed force.

So what has this got to do with IICSA? Everything and nothing, as it turns out. A few people – myself included – have been arguing that the Church of England is not a competent body to run its own safeguarding any more. It cannot investigate, police and repair the manifest malfunctions and injustices that occur within its safeguarding. To be candid, the Church of England is too small and poorly resourced to really manage this well. Moreover, it cannot begin to address the changes in culture it needs to face, adopt and implement, if it is to run a holistic framework of safeguarding.

This is because problems in safeguarding do not just stem from some poor professionalism and meagre managerialism. They are rooted in warped attitudes to gender and sexuality; cultures of obeisance that do not challenge or question the competence of clergy and bishops, instead putting them on a pedestal; failures to invest in training for seminarians and clergy in the basics of law, good practices, and relevant social and psychological theory; patronising attitudes towards laity; and lazy, naïve assumptions about human nature. These things will not be fixed by hiring a few more safeguarding officers. The problem runs far deeper, and extends far wider.

The Church of England has not even begun to reckon with the ecclesial ethos and traditions that offered the best petri-dishes for developing and growing cultures of abuse. For decades, it has been easy for the church to point the finger of blame at liberals for lax standards and moral lapses. But the cultures of sexual abuse grew most successfully in traditionalist strains of Anglo-Catholicism (e.g. Bishop Peter Ball) and Biblicist strains of Conservative Evangelicalism (e.g. John Smyth of Iwerne Camps). There are common denominators between these two ecclesial cultures. They deny women equality. They are squeamish about sexuality. They sacralise ambiguity. They put their leaders on unimpeachable pedestals. The worst abuses flourish in the cultures that are self-righteous.

The recent Gibb Report and the Carlile Report (dealing respectively with quite different controversies surrounding Bishop Peter Ball and Bishop George Bell) are both damning of the practice of the Church of England's handling of safeguarding, the role of bishops in providing leadership and oversight, and the competence of the National Safeguarding Team. Both reports relay that the Church of England is simply not up to the job.

Perhaps there is no real shame in finally admitting this. Why should the Church of England be an omnicompetent body? The Church of England used to run orphanages, teacher training colleges, social and medical care centres, and more besides – including levying and collecting local taxes. But no longer. Moreover, the Church of England no longer even runs schools in the way that it used to, preserving its dwindling influence in education more indirectly through governance and the shaping of a more benign, implicit ethos. But direct responsibility for schooling – and with it the power and authority to educate – was ceded long ago. These changes were all part of a culture-shift and secularisation that began long ago in the nineteenth century.

The Church of England wants to remain as a religious, civic and unrestricted body that can serve the nation. But it simply lacks the resources to be a public utility in a way that is accountable and transparent. For this reason – among many others – the Church of England would position itself better in the public domain if it made itself subject to those norms that govern other aspects of public life. For example, signing up unequivocally, for equality legislation that addresses gender and sexuality, so ending its own 'opt out' clauses that permit it to discriminate in the name of theology, or offer protection to dissenting minority ecclesial traditions.

In the same way, the Church of England could do worse than place itself under a new form of safeguarding regulation, free and independent from paying homage to ecclesial patronage and deferring to episcopal authority. Such a regulator could firmly bind the Church to principles of law and justice first, be thoroughly forensic with its investigative powers, and have the authority to call the Church to account. This would be far better for the Churches, as they are, instead, (inevitably) always trying to read cases of sexual abuse, harassment and safeguarding in a bifurcating, binocular way, with one lens always firmly trained on reputational risk.

The experience of watching the Church of England at IICSA – represented by the Diocese of Chichester – has left many of us with a profound sense of despair, and even hopelessness. IICSA gave a platform to some slow, steady, measured cross-examination of witnesses for the institution of the church, which in turn revealed their gross incompetence, shoddy amateurism and some shady nepotism. Their testimony highlighted an ecclesial culture that sought to keep up appearances, keep the show on the road, and protect its reputation at all costs.

The victims, and any kind of deep and broad inquiries relating to and leading to truth, emerged as being of very minor importance to the Church of England. It is hard not to feel ashamed of this – of being part of a body that has behaved with such callous and calculated indifference towards victims, whilst insisting on due deference to itself in public. Meanwhile, one can only admire the forensic cross-examination done by the women driving the inquiry, and their patient, point-by-point excavation of the deep culture of sexism and misogyny that clearly compacted with Chichester's paedophile problems.

A number of bishops and church leaders spoke openly last week about their sense of shame at the abuses, expressing sorrow and contrition. There were apologies. This, alas, is not enough. It won't be sufficient to change the culture that has produced and concealed the abuses. And there is no strategy in place to connect to the aspirations lightly sketched by some church leaders. The absence of strategy is telling. It is one thing to say 'we need to get this right in future', and quite another thing to face why it went wrong in the first place, then marshal resources to challenge prevailing cultures, and replace them with a more holistic range of policies and practices. I see little sign of this in the Church of England; few resources for it, and very little leadership that will take responsibility for the tasks that lie ahead.

This article has had little to say about the experiences and voices of victims. But in reflecting and writing, I have become aware that the abuses that victims suffer at the hands of the Church will go unheeded unless the church hands over its power and authority in safeguarding to a genuinely free and independent regulatory body. This is the only way that victims will be able to get the justice they deserve. It is the only way the churches can begin to rebuild public trust. Ultimately, this now an argument about a change of culture: one that many of us now believe is an urgent priority for churches. Without it, I fear for both victims and institution alike.

The Very Rev Professor Martyn Percy *is Dean of Christ Church, Oxford, and Vice President of Modern Church.*

Chapter 27

Joining the Dots: Theology and Culture that Breed Clergy Abuse of Women

Christina Rees

In over 25 years of campaigning for the ordination of women in the Church of England, I became aware of a number of themes that were frequently repeated in the arguments against ordaining women. In my brief contribution to this timely, necessary and courageous book, I would like to highlight just a few of the elements, over and above human fallenness and sinfulness, that I believe have contributed to a culture in which the sexual abuse of women by clergy has been able to persist.

These elements have to do with what we think about God and ourselves as the people of God; the patriarchal nature of the institutional Church; the dominance of male language in our liturgies; a culture that seems to breed an attitude of clericalism; and a fear, and at times, hatred, of women and female sexuality.

Together, these things have created a climate in which women have had to struggle against damaging stereotypes and projections, such as the idea that women secretly want to be raped, and in which women, and men, have been rendered vulnerable to abuse from clergy.

I am hopeful that this is changing and that policies and practices are now being put in place that will make it more difficult for clergy to abuse children or adults. I would also like to think that as we acknowledge what has happened in the past and repent of how we have allowed certain understandings of God to be used to justify abuse, and how we have put the interests of the institution above the interests of the victims, we will be more able to grow into the kind of Church in which this abuse will become increasingly unlikely.

On 20 November 2012 a vote in General Synod on opening the episcopate to women was narrowly lost. One of the speeches strongly against the principle of allowing women to be bishops centred on the immutable hierarchy within the Trinity. The speaker, the Rev Angus Macleay of Rochester Diocese, argued that, as the Son is eternally subordinate to the Father, so women are likewise subordinate to men. To permit women to have spiritual authority over men would be to introduce into the orders, and order, of the Church of England a pattern contrary to the very nature of God. He was, of course, expounding what is now widely considered to be the heresy of subordinationism.

Angus Macleay is from the conservative Evangelical wing of the Church, but at the other end of the spectrum traditionalist Anglo-Catholics also spoke against ordaining women as priests and bishops, often arguing that women *couldn't* be ordained. (In the early 1990s, at the time of the debates about ordaining women as priests, one cleric commented: "You can no more ordain a woman than you can ordain a pork pie!") If priests are representatives of Christ, then women cannot represent Christ because they are not male. These and other theological views, including various understandings of the nature of the Eucharist and of Apostolic tradition also led traditionalists to hold that it was not possible for women to be ordained.

If someone does not believe that the very Being of God embraces and includes the feminine in the way that God embraces and includes the masculine, then it is perhaps not surprising that women are seen as inferior to men. If the Bible is read simplistically and not subjected to hermeneutical rigour, and if past traditions that held discriminatory views of women are not critically examined, then women will continue to be seen as inferior to men, and therefore what they may, or may not, want will be deemed to be unimportant.

Of course, most conservative Evangelicals and traditionalist Anglo-Catholics would have denied that their views of God implied that women are inferior to men, but that is not how they came across, and that is not the effect they had on the Church overall. That it took over 20 years between accepting that women could be ordained as priests, to agreeing to consecrate women as bishops shows the tenacious hold that discriminatory views of women and the power of patriarchy had within the Church and its structures.

The maleness of God was frequently underscored by how people would talk about God or about male priests, most notably with Evangelicals endlessly addressing God as 'Father God' in prayers and worship songs, and with Anglo-Catholics typically referring to male priests as 'Father'.

Dr Margaret Kennedy, founder of MACSAS (Minister and Clergy Sexual Abuse Survivors) and a leading expert on sexual abuse by clergy in the Roman Catholic Church, has talked for many years with hundreds of women survivors. In a talk given in 2003 she argued that "a male God teaches female children that males are superior to women, more powerful than women, and more God-like than women." She cited comments made by women survivors of clergy abuse which made an explicit link between what women were taught about God and the abuse they experienced.

One said, "I was taught that God was my father in heaven and that my own father was like God on earth. I was terrified of God." Another stated, "Father for me is the most frightening name for God I can think of."

Over and above what the women had been taught, their abuse as children led them to form some appallingly tragic views of God:

> I figured God couldn't love me – I was going to hell no matter what I did, so it didn't matter whether I lived or died.

And

> I thought that I must have deserved it. Why would God do this if I didn't deserve it?

These may be examples from the Roman Catholic Church, but they could equally well have been said by women survivors of clergy abuse in the Church of England.

Margaret Kennedy also found that while most of the women she spoke to still had faith in God, unsurprisingly many had problems with the Church. She also discovered that women survivors of clergy sexual abuse could be found in all the mainstream Christian denominations, as well as in those not in the mainstream.

In December 2018 the Fort Worth *Star-Telegram* broke the story of 412 allegations of sexual misconduct in 187 Independent Fundamental Baptist churches across the United States and Canada. Evidently, the churches had been covering up the abuse for decades, silencing the victims and allowing the abusers to retain their positions of leadership in the Independent Fundamental Baptist church network.

In commenting on the story, the Rev Gricel Medina, a theologian, counsellor and minister in an independent Evangelical church that ordains women, wrote, "The problems we're seeing in our churches are cultural problems, and cultural problems flow out of theological and ideological brokenness." (The full article can be found at: https://www.cbeinternational.org/blogs/hundreds-abuse-allegations-baptist-churches-what-now.)

From her experience of many years of counselling women who have been abused by clergy, Medina, observes that:

> It's becoming increasingly clear that systemic abuse is the inevitable conclusion of authoritarian theology, absolute trust in pastors and the singular control granted spiritual leaders ... Spiritual leaders have a lot of influence over how their congregants view God. If they teach about a wrathful, authoritarian God, it's very difficult for believers to question an abusive, authoritarian representative.

Pope Francis called a Conference on Clerical Sexual Abuse held in February 2019 to address the issue of the sex abuse crisis in the Roman Catholic Church worldwide. One of the organisers of the Conference was Fr Hans Zollner, a Jesuit priest, theologian, psychologist and a leading expert on sexual abuse in the Catholic Church.

In an Open Letter to Fr Hans Zollner dated 30 December 2018, Catholic Church Reform International called for, among other things: the eradication of the 'culture of clericalism'; the inclusion of lay people at all levels of decision making; independent tribunals to be set up with a majority of lay experts to examine accusations of abuse; women to be included at all levels of ministry in the Church; a remodelling of priestly formation; priestly celibacy to be made optional; and for victims/survivors of sexual abuse to be involved in all deliberations, especially before any concrete decisions are taken.

There is a growing awareness in many denominations that sexual abuse by clergy is made possible by a number of inter-connected factors. One of the most frequent obstacles in talking with members of the Church of England about ordaining women was their assumption that the people in charge had to be male. Even in a country in which the monarch (and Supreme Governor of the Church of England) is female; where we had elected a female Prime Minister; and where people were well accustomed to female doctors, lawyers, teachers and so on; it still unsettled some people to conceive of a woman holding spiritual authority.

For a woman to occupy positions of so called 'secular' authority was fine but for women to hold spiritual authority was seen by some as usurping the male role and by others as being almost blasphemous to God. Unpacking those views and others like them uncovered a host of disturbing views, some that can be traced back to past centuries in which women were variously thought to be ravenous sexual predators, unable to bear God's image in their bodies or minds, polluted and polluting, or even barely human.

Contrast this legacy with the story of God creating humankind, where the inclusion and equality of women and men is beautifully evident:

> Let us make humankind in our image, according to our likeness ... So God cre-
> ated humankind in his image, in the image of God he created them; male and
> female he created them. (Genesis 1. 26a, 27, NRSV)

Such disordered views also make a travesty of our understanding of what it means to be baptised into Christ:

> There is no longer Jew or Greek, there is no longer slave or free, there is no
> longer male and female; for all of you are one in Christ Jesus. (Galatians 3. 28,
> NRSV)

Even after women had been ordained as priests, there was a telling experience when 20 senior women (18 priests and two laywomen) were invited to attend a meeting of the College of Bishops. The guest speaker was Cardinal Walter Kaspar, who had been asked to speak about why he thought it would be wrong for the Church of England to consecrate women as bishops. Following his talk, which was somewhat galling for the women (as were many such talks), the bishops spoke about how uncomfortable they had been listening to the Cardinal with the women present.

This was a strong and widespread reaction. It was clear that the men would not have been so sensitive to the views being expressed by the Cardinal if women had not been present. An institution that is patriarchal, intentionally or otherwise, is an institution in which women will be seen as both 'other' and 'lesser', or, at times, not 'seen' at all.

I am aware this book has been assembled against the backdrop of the ongoing investigations of the Independent Inquiry into Child Sexual Abuse. In July 2019, as this book is published, there will be nearly two weeks of public hearings specifically about abuse in the Church of England (https://www.iicsa.org.uk/investigations/investigation-in-to-failings-by-the-anglican-church). With all the stories of abuse that have already come out, it is distressing to think that more such stories are likely to be revealed. But acknowledging what has gone on is necessary for the hope of healing and restitution for those who have been abused and for the transformation of our Church.

One of the ongoing challenges of the Church of England will be to identify those views of women, men and children which continue to undermine the full humanity of women or women's ability to bear the image of God and to expose these as no longer being consistent with our understanding of God and of humankind.

The breadth of the Church of England is one of its greatest qualities and has helped to create some of the most wonderful things about our Church. Where it is lived out, there is the experience of mutual respect, the gracious tolerance, even celebration, of difference and genuine spiritual humility. But this quality has a shadow side, as it has been used to provide cover for some seeking to undermine the true breadth of the Church and of Anglicanism, in order to introduce more rigid, hierarchical, patriarchal and authoritarian ways of thinking; ways which are likely to feed a culture that distorts the full humanity of women.

Looking ahead, I would like to think that incidents of clergy sexual abuse of women and children will fall as more women are appointed as bishops and as more lay and ordained women are included on key boards and committees and in other in decision making bodies.

I would like to think that from now on the Church of England will include more women, including younger women and women of colour, on any group or commission that explores the nature of God or that is asked to look at liturgical language. We must find more ways of addressing and describing God that include the feminine if we are ever to counteract the view of an all-male God, or at least, of a God who prefers males and in whom God's image is considered to be more fully visible.

I would like to think that theological educators will take special care in the formation of clergy to ensure that they hold views of the priesthood and laity that do not result in a slide into a sense of superiority with the consequent dangers of clericalism. And for their part, I would like to think that the laity could be helped not to place frankly un-Christian expectations or projections onto clergy.

Many of the calls being made in the Roman Catholic Church to be discussed at the Conference on Clerical Sexual Abuse are similar to ones that need to be made in the Church of England. The brokenness of our Church is only part of the brokenness of all Churches, as they expose the disfiguring reality of clergy sexual abuse and struggle to transform themselves into a more true, authentic and healthy Body of Christ; one in which:

> Speaking the truth in love, we must grow up in every way into him who is the head, into Christ, from whom the whole body, joined and knitted together by every ligament with which it is equipped, as each part is working properly, promotes the body's growth in building itself up in love. (Ephesians 4.15–16, NRSV).

In such a body there can be no abuse.

Christina Rees is a writer, broadcaster, speaker, preacher and practical theologian working primarily with issues of women and religion

and contemporary Christian spirituality. She was a member of General Synod for 25 years and a founder member of the Archbishops' Council. Christina is also a coach and communications consultant and part-time lay chaplain in a prep school in North Norfolk. She was awarded a CBE in 2015 for services to the Church of England.

Chapter 28

Enduring Cruelty

Graham Sawyer

"Then said Jesus, Father, forgive them; for they know not what they do. And they parted his raiment, and cast lots."

The following statement was sent by email to every member of General Synod (as well as all other bishops and archdeacons) on the eve of their meeting in London in February 2018:

> "As one of the two people about whom Bishop Peter Ball pleaded guilty with respect to historic sexual offences I forgive Bishop Ball from my heart for what he did to me and wish him no ill will whatsoever. I also have absolutely no doubt about the personal integrity, competence and compassion of Bishop Peter Hancock as lead bishop for safeguarding.
>
> That said, the enduringly cruel and sadistic treatment I have faced from the National Safeguarding Team in Church House and others in the Church of England hierarchy makes what Bishop Ball did to me pale into insignificance: this comes as a result, I believe, of a deep-rooted narcissism.
>
> We cannot move forward as a church with respect to truth, reconciliation and peace until the National Safeguarding Team is abolished: it is, in short, wicked in the way it treats survivors/victims of sexual abuse as I know only too well from my own experience."

Three bishops, one member of the House of Clergy and three members of the House of Laity wrote in reply: this level of response does, I believe, indicate the degree to which the Church of England, in practice, responds to sexual abuse and the treatment of victims and survivors by the Church of England. After the many years of revelations of sexual abuse as well as the conviction of Bishop Peter Ball one would perhaps think that there might have been an explosion of consciousness by the leaders of the Church of England. But alas it has still to take place and one might be forgiven for thinking if it ever will.

The way survivors of clergy-perpetrated sexual abuse (and that perpetrated by other church officials) have been treated by those at the highest levels in the Church of England is often felt by those of us on the receiving end to be enduringly cruel. I know this from my own experience and also from the testimonies of so many others who have contacted me. It has been a similar experience in other branches of the Anglican Communion as evidenced, for example, in Australia, where so much has emerged from the Royal Commission Into Institutionalised Responses to Child Sexual Abuse (to which I gave evidence). Bishop Greg Thompson, former Bishop of Newcastle in New South Wales and himself a victim of clergy sexual abuse when he was a young man, described the treatment meted out to him when he reported his abuse as an "ecclesiastical protection racket". It is no different in England, many of us feel.

There is something in the culture of Anglicanism, perhaps based on its historic connexions with the Establishment in England and the hierarchical structure of the Church, that causes this. Until the truth is exposed reconciliation and redemption can never take place. If we do not deal with the past then the trauma, the disability and the pain will continue for many people and for many years. Reconciliation and peace can only truly come about by means of the truth becoming public. Yet there seems to be no desire for this to take place. Perhaps it is as a result of a sub-conscious contempt for the victims of an embarrassing crime, combined with a mistaken belief that the preservation of the reputation and standing of the institution of the church is always more important than any individual's well-being? At heart though, a lot of people have become disillusioned with the Church of England because it has so often been a poor advertisement for the reality of the loving Jesus and the response of the hierarchy has clearly lacked love. The Church of England has been far too deeply concerned about its power, its wealth and its status. It continues to insist upon a level of respect that it has not earned and does not deserve. It also continues to be woefully silent with regard to real change, not least with respect to the fundamental safety and care of children and vulnerable adults.

The solution to the crisis of confidence in the Church of England with respect to safeguarding is simple. First, there needs to be an explosion of consciousness by clergy and laity alike that this problem is not going away, and indeed is worsening. Second, in order to introduce a hitherto absent transparency and credibility, there needs to be independent external monitoring and management of safeguarding (this was recommended by the Australian Royal Commission and has already been put in place by the Anglican Church of Australia). It is in the interest of victims/survivors as well as the Church of England as an institution that this takes place – sooner rather than later.

Evidence given by bishops, archbishops and national safeguarding managers at the Independent Inquiry into Child Sexual abuse have shown the complete inadequacy of church leadership to go on monitoring and policing itself. When one lay leader in Church House was asked about the adverse comments of survivors concerning the organisation they head, the response seemed to be that the problem was more one of managing expectations of survivors than having any real empathy or compassion – well that it is certainly how it seemed to me.

The Church of England has covered up child sexual abuse for years and clearly has an attitudinal problem that shows few signs of abating. The current corporate managers (for that is surely what they are) appear too smug to realise their own narcissism with respect to dealing with this on-going scandal. In my view there is a corporate personality disorder in the Church of England that attacks those who are perceived to threat the institution and power of those who head it. Unless a genuine change of attitude, action and accountability is forthcoming, the fear is that more people could take their lives, and more people will have their faith destroyed.

If a Church of England behaving in this way had been a secular institution it may, rather like the *News of the World* newspaper, have been shut down. Let us hope that those who have failed so spectacularly and with such devastating consequences in their leadership and management of the Church of England, with respect to the treatment of survivors of sexual abuse, can have the decency to step aside and let others take their place.

Graham Sawyer is an Anglican priest and a survivor.

Chapter 29

The Lessons of the Independent Inquiry into Child Sexual Abuse

Richard Scorer

A saga of "religious exceptionalism, stupidity, incompetence, lying, dumping responsibility at every level including the highest, and delusions of grandeur". This was Bishop Alan Wilson's description of the three weeks of hearings into the Church of England diocese of Chichester, which took place at the Independent Inquiry into Child Sexual Abuse (IICSA) in March 2018. Wilson's conclusion: "Bishops have to be accountable. And not just to themselves."

Anyone who sat through the hearings would certainly recognise that picture. Burnt files. Former Bishop Wallace Benn refusing to acknowledge safeguarding failings because "his primary concern was for the honour of God". A serial paedophile thinking that "he was able to deny all the charges against him because he believed he had been forgiven by God, his slate wiped clean". Church lawyers interfering with the wording of apologies. Shirley Hosgood, Chichester's former safeguarding adviser, explaining how she resigned because of the diocese's indifference to safeguarding work. And revelations that in the Robert Coles case "a diocesan bishop, an area bishop, an archdeacon and two safeguarding advisers knew that he had admitted to some of the matters about which he had been questioned by the police, and none of them told the police". These are just a few examples from a long and depressing litany of what must surely be seen by an independent observer as malice and incompetence.

One could list many more. After three weeks, it was obvious that the Church of England is beset by deep-seated cultural and structural problems which continue to put many children and vulnerable adults at risk, and which continue to deny fair redress to survivors. The question I posed at the end of the hearings was this: can these problems be solved by the Church itself, or is this achievable only through external intervention?

In my view, part of the answer to that question comes from looking at the history of events in Chichester itself. Safeguarding in the diocese of Chichester is now better than it was: it could scarcely fail to be. But the history reveals an indisputable fact: the exposure of the scandals in Chichester, and the changes to safeguarding which have followed on from them, came about overwhelmingly because of pressure from outside the Church.

At every turn in the Chichester saga, the Church was reactive rather than proactive: reactive to pressure from survivors, and pressure from the media. What made the difference in Chichester was an exceptionally determined survivor campaigner in Phil Johnson, and a dedicated and tenacious journalist in Colin Campbell. The internal church memos which came to light in March prove without question that but for their efforts, the appalling scandal of child abuse in Chichester – and its systematic cover-up – would have remained hidden from view.

But while Chichester has its own peculiarities, in terms of the prevalence of sex offending it will be no different from any other Church of England diocese. Every diocese has a Roy Cotton and a Colin Pritchard, and probably quite a few of them: these offenders are everywhere. Yet the reality also is that unlike Chichester not every diocese has a Phil Johnson or a Colin Campbell. In the future, the protection of children cannot be left to uniquely determined individuals.

If the tenacity of campaigners and the media was critical to effecting change in Chichester and in the wider Church, so too has been the very existence of IICSA itself. We saw the role of IICSA in forcing change in the Church during the March 2018 hearing when the inquiry's barrister identified a local parish church where a vicar had been convicted for sexual offences yet there was no safeguarding policy on the website – a remarkable omission which was rapidly remedied after it was put to a clearly embarrassed Bishop Warner in evidence. A failing addressed under the glare of a hearing: this was a small but telling vignette. We also heard in the hearing that the church might consider changing its language around the duty to report allegations – changing the word 'should' to the word 'must'. Again, this was a change only conceded – if it happens at all – under the IICSA spotlight after a question from one of the inquiry's panel members. But IICSA will not last forever: as Edina Carmi said in her evidence, what will there be to keep up the pressure for change after the inquiry has finished?

There was much talk from senior Church leaders in the March hearings about culture change in the Church. Bishop Hancock talked about changing hearts and minds. No one can doubt his genuine desire to do so. But the reality, of course, is that cultural change, if it happens at all, is a decades-long process. There are some good people in the Church: Bishop Hancock has always been empathetic and caring in his dealings with survivors, and Colin Perkins has done outstanding work in Chichester. But there are too many others, especially in the senior layer, who pay lip service to safeguarding but who in truth see it as at best an irritant and at worst a serious threat to their own authority and power.

At the July 2018 General Synod, just before the safeguarding debate, we heard a long homily from Archbishop Sentamu, who is himself seriously compromised in his dealings with survivors. After paying the usual lip service to the importance of safeguarding, he proceeded to expound at length on the centrality of forgiveness to the Christian message – without even a hint of awareness of the deeply problematic role of 'forgiveness' in church abuse scandals. I despair at his lack of awareness, and his intellectual shallowness. This is the second most senior bishop in the Church of England. Further afield, it is true that some of the bishops who obstructed safeguarding in Chichester have retired. But they mentored a generation of priests and their attitudes haven't simply gone away.

The sexist attitudes which underpinned the scandal still persist: as Archbishop Welby accepted in his evidence, there is still a level of misogyny in the church. There is still a very large gender imbalance. Hence the attitude we saw from Bishop Benn – the attitude that regarded the incredibly mild-mannered Shirley Hosgood as "aggressive" and having a chip on her shoulder because she dared to question his male headship. We can be sure that this mentality is still alive and well in many places.

When Archbishop Welby talked about cultural change, what struck me most was his impotence in being able to effect it – or at least the serious limitations on his power. He can't direct his bishops. He can't change what happens in theological colleges where culture is implanted. And he can't change the very muddled and conflicted attitude to homosexuality in the Church, not just because of the wider Anglican Communion but because he himself believes that homosexuality is a sin. Archbishop Welby talked about training and trying to build a new theology. But it was very telling that when he gave a secular example of cultural change – drunk driving and how that was tackled – he was actually talking about a problem that was dealt with not primarily through training, but through the law: by tougher laws and stronger law enforcement. In other words, a problem which was tackled using hard powers, which are exactly what he doesn't have. In his evidence Bishop Hancock also talked about developing a theology of safeguarding. I hope he does; but the reality is that ideas of this kind will take decades to bear fruit in changing behaviour, if they do at all.

We heard in March about the structural problems in the Church: the unaccountable power of bishops; the autonomy of dioceses; the slow and cumbersome nature of the Clergy Discipline Measure (CDM) process, and how unfit for purpose it is in safeguarding terms. But there was no sign at the hearing of any serious plan to start to tackle, let alone remedy, any of these deep-seated problems. And save for the plan published before the July Synod for a victims' ombudsman – of which more below – there has been none since. Tellingly, even at the March hearing (for which the church had four years to prepare) there was a complete lack of data to enable us to assess action taken under the CDM. Bishop Hancock was unsure as to whether there has ever been a prosecution for failure to have "due regard for House of Bishops safeguarding guidance": clearly a very unsatisfactory answer from the lead safeguarding Bishop. As Edina Carmi said, structure should adapt to the needs of safeguarding but the reality is that the church is fiddling around with a structure which is fundamentally unsound. Unsurprisingly, the National Adviser on Safeguarding was reluctant to acknowledge this, but his head-in-the-sand approach does not change the reality.

In summary, this is a Church with profound cultural and structural problems, but with a dearth of real levers to change them. Change, if it happens at all, will take generations, and safeguarding is far too urgent for that. Children and vulnerable adults, and the survivors who have been failed over so many years, do not have the luxury of time. And in any case the history of events in Chichester teaches us that nothing really changes in the Church of England without external pressure.

So the overwhelming lesson of the previous hearings is that in future there has to be genuinely independent oversight to make the church honest and to keep it so – a permanent set of mechanisms to protect children and vulnerable adults and to ensure independent investigation and redress for survivors. Put simply, the church cannot be allowed to carry on marking its own homework.

As I told the Inquiry, one of these mechanisms is mandatory reporting: the requirement that knowledge or suspicions of abuse must be reported to the statutory authorities, and with a legal penalty for failure to do so.

Mandatory reporting would obviously apply to all regulated activities, not simply to the Church of England. The case for it has already been made powerfully by others and is supported by international experience. As Canon Rupert Bursell said in the hearings, just as we require it with money laundering and terrorism, so we should require it with child abuse (and without any exemption for the confessional). If there remained any doubt about the need for mandatory reporting, it has now been extinguished by the recent exposure of the widespread and lamentable shortcomings in the Church's 2010 Past Cases Review (PCR). But given that the need for mandatory reporting goes well beyond the Church of England I will say no more about it here, save to highlight that irrespective of whether the law is changed, the clear evidence of the hearings is that Church policies do not currently mandate the external reporting of abuse allegations. A painstaking analysis by Mandate Now made this clear, and it was implicitly confirmed by Graham Tilby in his evidence when he used the words "should" and "must" interchangeably, as if they mean the same thing. Plainly they do not. If the Church of England is serious about safeguarding, then it needs to cut the managerial voodoo and inject clarity into its reporting policies as a matter of urgency.

Turning to independent oversight mechanisms which are specific to the Church of England, I want to be clear: I am not proposing that safeguarding itself be removed from the Church. In my view that would not be practicable, and morally the Church has to own the responsibility to put in place effective safeguarding rather than passing the buck to others. But there is an urgent need for a set of genuinely independent oversight mechanisms covering five aspects: diocesan audit and case review; investigation of victim and whistleblower complaints; victim redress; and clergy discipline and risk assessment. Considerable work will be required to develop these mechanisms. For now, I highlight two points.

Firstly, so far as diocesan audit is concerned, the most recent paper from the Church – released in June 2018, in advance of the Synod safeguarding session in July – confirms that Church continues to regard the SCIE (Social Care Institute for Excellence) audits as constituting a sufficient form of external audit. The reality, of course, is that the SCIE audits do not adequately fulfill this function. They are not frequent enough; they are time limited; they are done on terms set by the church; they haven't involved survivor input (a point made by Minister and Clergy Sexual Abuse Survivors [MACSAS] for several years, but only now being addressed); and of course the Church decides whether they happen or not.

None of this is a criticism of SCIE. Edina Carmi herself acknowledged the limitations of the audit process. But there is a fundamental problem with external audit where that audit is designed and chosen by the organisation being overseen: a problem illustrated in the hearings when we heard how Andrew Nunn, a senior official at Lambeth Palace, suggested that Dame Elizabeth Butler-Sloss was a good choice to do an external report because she was likely to be sympathetic ("Bishop Hind knows her and thinks he and [Bishop] Benn will be safe in her hands"). A revealing comment which demonstrates that when procuring external oversight, the Church will always be minded to choose a form of oversight thought likely to be sympathetic.

Genuinely independent audit cannot be selected by the Church and organised on terms congenial to it. To put it another way: not only can the Church not be allowed to mark its own homework, but it also won't be good enough if the homework ends up being marked by somebody else but the Church is still choosing the marker; and the Church still gets to decide the terms on which they're doing the marking; and how long the marking goes on for. Future diocesan audit not only has to be much more extensive than it currently is, but it has to be genuinely independent and permanent.

Secondly, so far as investigation of complaints is concerned, it must be obvious by now that any system must have public confidence and especially survivor confidence. The reality is that survivors will not come forward with complaints unless they have a basic confidence in the machinery of investigation. Survivors need to be certain that complaints will be taken seriously; investigated impartially and without the conflicts of interest that can arise in close knit and closed church communities; and investigated in a timely fashion. Lack of survivor confidence in Church institutions – especially the National Safeguarding Team – is now deep seated and very palpable.

Archbishop Welby stated in his evidence that "you have to keep coming back to what works for the survivors". The simple fact is that survivors have consistently said that what works for survivors is independent investigation of complaints. The June 2018 Synod paper talks about the idea of an "independent complaints ombudsman". This is a start – it is possibly the most positive aspect of the June paper – but probably still an inadequate one. "Independent" is not defined (and the Church and survivors may well have different notions of what this word means). There is no timescale attached to the proposal. Despite the manifest failings of the CDM process, there is no proposal to hand the clergy discipline aspect over to an independent body. And the paper fails to address the vexed issue of redress, where far too many survivors have experienced the handling of cases by EIG as a re-traumatising insult compounding the abuse itself.

As I said at the end of the March 2018 hearing: survivors have lost years of their lives trying to challenge the Church and get the Church to change. It would be a tragedy if another generation of survivors have to undergo the same experience. Only genuinely independent oversight will have any prospect of ensuring that future generations of children and vulnerable adults are spared the same fate, and we need to ensure that this is now put in place.

Richard Scorer *is Head of Abuse Law at Slater and Gordon and represents victims and survivors at Independent Inquiry into Child Sexual Abuse (IICSA). He is Vice President of the National Secular Society (NSS).*

Chapter 30

General Synod, Do Your Job

Martin Sewell

My brothers and sisters in Christ,

How did we get here?

How did the rock upon which Christ founded his Church, intending it to be a place of welcome for the broken and the vulnerable, become the place that nurtured a nest of vipers, harming those who came to us in trust?

How did we, who succeeded to the responsibility of being the healing hands of Christ in the world, become so complicit in bestowing yet another kiss of betrayal?

Moreover, when the children bravely came and told us what was wrong, how did we come to turn them away and not recognise the truth when it was set before us? Why do we still struggle to listen and respond, so that once again, they feel rejected by our disinterest and hardness of heart?

Let me refine that thought; too often our victims feel sidelined because they ARE rejected by our disinterest and hardness of heart, especially when their complaints touch those of us who are still in positions of power, respect and influence in the Church of today.

The answers to these questions are probably very familiar.

Like the disciples before us we have been weak; we fled when we should have been brave, steadfast, and active. Like Pilate, we feared turbulence and criticism, so we washed our hands of responsibility. Like the High Priests, we were proud and defensive of our traditions and would not contemplate the idea of a beam in our own eye. We cared too much for the world's opinion and not enough for the truth, or for the welfare of those thirsting for wholeness and justice. We lacked Christ-like love and Christ-like grace.

Oscar Wilde was wrong. It was not homosexuality that was the sin that dare not speak its name, it was child abuse. The Bible is surprisingly silent on the subject. Horrific violence towards children is to be found there, but the idea of the child as an object of sexual desire and exploitation was seemingly so gross, so unthinkable, so discomforting, as to not make it into the narrative of sin, in any explicit manner. It was too shocking even to set down in the Holy Book, which, considering what depravity did make it into the text, ought to have alerted us.

Perhaps that absence of a text to be studied, asserted and defended, reveals a lack of prophetic imagination and confidence in the Holy Spirit as a force who leads us creatively, actively and challengingly in our age. Did we really need a "thou shalt not..." to figure out that Jesus requires us to act compassionately and quickly when we encounter the corruption of abuse and the cover-ups within our Church life? Yet when the children asked to share the bread of empathy, we gave them the stones of indifference and corporate inertia.

Un-named, the sin of child abuse festered under the radar in schools, children's homes and churches, and when detected it was passed over as a minor peccadillo, a temporary aberration under the stress of loneliness, separation, drink or temptation; sometimes we accepted the perpetrators' lie that temptation had been placed in the miscreants' path by "devious" victims pursuing a murky purpose of their own, as if containing the reputational damage to the institution was the greatest problem to be addressed. This sounds utterly shocking today, but it was only 30 years ago that such attitudes and understandings prevailed across all institutions. We forgave too readily and empathised too little with the implications for the vulnerable. To a worrying degree, in that latter respect, we still do.

Too often, when our victims dared to disclose, our institutional response seemed to echo the words and attitudes of their abusers. " Who is going to believe you?" "You're not important." "You are wasting your time." "Just go away quietly"...

As a young lawyer I began a steep learning curve; the development of my professional life coincided with the growing understanding of the true character of this crime. To begin with, I heard that "all children lie". You could hire Freudian psychiatrists who would tell the courts that all little girls fantasised about having sex with their fathers. I heard women lawyers speak of "breaking the victim" in the witness box; it was what passed for female empowerment in those not so far off days. It sounds glib to talk of a culture of denial but that is what it was, and we still suffer from the hangover of such attitudes to this day. Slowly we built a composite understanding of the complexity of the problem and we needed a multi-disciplinary approach to understand it. Police couldn't fix it on their own, nor social workers, lawyers, judges or psychiatrists, we had to all interact and we needed to listen to victims. This is why I distrust our reliance on the House of Bishops to be the primary agent of reform. "If they knew better – they'd do better" as Martin Luther King once proclaimed of an earlier hierarchy slow to address a glaring injustice.

Like a particularly challenging virus, the problems of abuse and our inadequate institutional responses morph and persist, constantly presenting new facets, and we always seem to show reluctance to respond quickly and decisively.

Another sin has become acceptable; "reputational management" has replaced true repentance as we accept the advice of insurers, PR men and professional bureaucrats rather than respond as sincerely grieving pastors. To often we have proffered the cold platitudes that "lessons have been learnt", "policies are being developed," and our "apologies" are still framed in the language of lawyers rather than penitents. What we have rarely heard is the direct testimony of our victims expressing a sense of being heard, embraced and healed by our responses. Individuals within the Church may model the sensitivity of our Lord but this rarely makes it through our corporate structures.

Because our Church is institutional, devolved, and Established, we are easily daunted at the seeming complexity of change. "These things take time" is an attractive alibi, as is the placing of too much faith in developing process. Good process is very necessary but, to a large extent, secondary to that modelled by Christ – who reached out with heartfelt love to the despondent.

So what is to be done?

Plainly, at every level of the Church we need to switch our "default mode" from defensiveness to empathetic listening. I have been listening for the past three years

I began my personal engagement with our shortcomings when I heard the Church explaining its actions in the case of the late Bishop George Bell, and found my professional hackles rising at the assertion of so much that I simply knew not to be true. I had spent 30 years working as a child protection lawyer; I knew poor practice when I saw it and began to say so.

What I did not foresee was how many victims of abusers would respond positively to someone whose only agenda was to "do things properly". They may have differing views on the truth behind the Bell case, but they immediately grasped that a Church that sacrificed good and fair practice for reputational protection was no friend of theirs. Justice for the accused and accuser alike are two sides of the same coin. Loaded dice are never excusable.

Stories began to be brought to me from across the spectrum. I hear from those whose abusers have been convicted, but who still thirst for justice and a sincere apology. I hear from the families of those investigated and cleared but who were nevertheless broken by the process. Some cases verge on the farcical, such as the person left in limbo for months because of alleged safeguarding issues arising out social media use; the Church "professionals" refusing to identify the allegedly worrying material on the grounds of "confidentiality" when the material belonged to the accused and had been published to the entire world. If you don't understand basic concepts you should not be doing the work.

One priest told of being instructed to rally support for a superior under suspicion, only to be subsequently made to look foolish after the guilty plea. He too is a victim of sorts; he feels foolish and sullied, his trust and good faith exploited by the institution he thought he could trust.

As we listen – if we listen – we hear a mixture of stories about our current and historic failings ranging from the incompetent to the mendacious.

From my own professional background a few practical suggestions might help take out many of our shortcomings. I spell these out because – extraordinary as it sounds – as far as I have been able to ascertain, the Church attempts to grapple with the medusa of abuse with a Safeguarding Establishment which does not employ a single specialist safeguarding lawyer on the team. Such specialists bring not only knowledge of the law (the easy part) but also the hinterland culture of good practice, comprehension of other disciplines, victim empathy, and confidence built on long experience.

It is as if we were to build a maternity hospital and refuse to employ any midwives. We would not be so blasé about such lack of specialised legal input if it touched upon the Church's investment or pension strategy. These are areas which our Bishops know are specialisms requiring length and depth of professional experience. But when it comes to safeguarding law they are happy to do half a job and offer to do their incompetent best. Surely we have learnt that the time for amateur-hour has passed. We need the decisions taken – or at the very least guided – by an independent multi-disciplinary body with victims seated round the table.

So here is my practical checklist for change; these are not expensive proposals:

1. Everyone engaging with our safeguarding teams should receive, within 7 days, a letter setting out the Church's understanding of the problem in clear terms; setting out who is responsible for advancing the matter; what the immediately foreseeable process will be; who to complain to; the best estimate for a time frame; and a clear assurance that regular updates will be given. A comprehensible leaflet explaining the processes involved and appeal rights should be sent to all relevant parties.

2. A protocol for consistent file management across the Dioceses, including an easily accessible chronology of events and actions, should be accurately compiled and maintained by the DSA (Diocesan Safeguarding Advisor) to facilitate outside monitoring.

3. A separate person from the file handler should devise and monitor a case management plan, which should be updated and communicated to all parties with regularity. That individual shall be responsible for ensuring timely compliance and answering questions as to progress.

4. Each complainant should have the opportunity to have a supportive advisor allocated within 14 days

5. Correspondence should be answered within 14 days; failure without proper explanation should be a disciplinary matter.

6. An Independent Ombudsman scheme should be established, and failure to comply with its recommendations should be a Clergy Discipline Offence.

7. Complaints against Bishops, NST and senior Church staff shall be independently adjudicated.

8. Victim liaison and support should be removed from the National Safeguarding Team and outsourced to a body disinterested in reputational issues, and overseen by a supervisory body including significant victim representatives.

Last year the booklet *We asked for bread you gave us stones* (http://abuselaw.co.uk/wp-content/uploads/2018/02/Stones-not-Bread.pdf) collated the experience of some of our victims and presented us with a devastating critique of our current stewardship. One of its contributors told me he had surveyed 72 victims asking them to score our National Safeguarding Team for their empathy towards those we have failed on a scale of 1 to 10. They received an aggregate score of zero.

Even allowing a degree of suspicion for the weaknesses of self-selecting samples, the picture emerges of a crisis of confidence in our Church safeguarding establishment. My own concerns are founded upon a realisation that our current structures and culture allow neither the Archbishop of Canterbury, nor the lead bishop for Safeguarding to exercise decisive executive leadership even where they see the need for it.

For what it is worth, I believe that both men are sincere and committed to meeting the needs and expectations of our victims, but that our structures and culture consistently militate against the urgent reform that is needed. We reform at a glacial pace.

The set of proposals presented to the members of General Synod in July 2018 came forward without the matters ever having been offered for debate in advance. We talk the language of 'transparency and accountability', but the representative body of the Church seemed to be managed, some say cynically.

We were not allowed to debate the Carlile Report into the poor handling of the Bishop Bell complaint. We have not been asked for our reactions to the shocking disclosures heard at the Independent Inquiry into Child Sexual Abuse (IICSA), nor the Singleton Report. Such reluctance implies weakness and insecurity when a more confident institution would initiate and welcome robust debate. The Church's critics wish to see it strengthened, not destroyed.

Until the 2018 York Synod the Church had never invited victims to talk directly to us and answer questions. It preferred the safety of pre-recorded selected testimony being played to us to offer a semblance of engagement, rather than the risky, raw, real thing.

York saw a step forward. Our leadership dared to make itself vulnerable and those listening to our accusers undoubtedly found the process uncomfortable. They nevertheless showed moral courage in facing the accusers and began the difficult task of rebuilding confidence and trust. Some of the sins were those of past office holders, but they were still hard to hear. All involved acknowledged that in listening to survivors the right thing had been done and the process of catharsis had begun.

As a comparatively new member of the General Synod, I am increasingly aware that for years the ruling body to which I have been elected has itself been weak, complacent, slow; uninterested in taking the victims seriously and reforming our safeguarding processes with the support of those with the experience and expertise to do so. It is time for that to change. We need to build within General Synod a healthy culture of active questioning and sympathetic scepticism. We must no more be considered a rubber stamp, but make ourselves open to hear victims from our various constituencies, and to bring their stories and grievances to the debating chamber.

At IICSA Archbishop Justin gave an important lead, telling us that the time for deference has passed. He is right. We should show him respect and take him at his word.

General Synod too must do its job.

Martin Sewell *is a member of General Synod for the Rochester Diocese and a retired Child Protection Solicitor.*

Chapter 31

Safeguarding Policy at a Crossroads

Josephine Stein

The Church of England stands at a crossroads. How did we get to where we are now? Where do we go from here?

Church of England safeguarding policy was first put together in the early 1990s by the then Bishop of Bath and Wells, Jim Thompson. The emphasis was on responding to any allegation of clerical sexual abuse by contacting the Church's insurers as a matter of urgency. The ground was laid for a confrontational, legalistic approach to safeguarding managed by lawyers, administrators and insurers, discouraging pastoral responses that might have been seen to compromise formal proceedings.

In 1996, a General Synod Working Party chaired by Alan Hawker produced a review of the 1963 Ecclesiastical Jurisdiction Measure's procedures for clergy discipline. Designed to address the overly complex, time consuming, expensive and damaging system of consistory courts, this report recommends that complaints 'must always be in writing' and that the burden of proof of an ecclesiastical offence needs to be 'beyond all reasonable doubt'. This may explain why, according to archdeacons, the Clergy Discipline Measure of 2003 (CDM) in practice applied evidentiary standards comparable to those used in criminal proceedings. And the procedures associated with the CDM became even more burdensome, complex, intimidating, time consuming, expensive and damaging, particularly to survivors of clerical sexual abuse, than the consistory court system it was designed to replace.

Church leaders were advised that to offer any apology to survivors of ecclesiastical abuse would be tantamount to accepting liability. Direct contact with survivors was discouraged. The Church used avoidance behaviour, proceduralism and various barriers and obstacles to frustrate attempts by survivors to be heard.

Once the Compensation Act (2006) came into force, apologies began to flow. Most came from senior Church leaders who hadn't met the survivor, didn't know about the abuse in any detail and were accompanied by offers to pray for the survivor as if this provided closure. A priest would never absolve a sinner on the basis of a confession made by another person on their behalf. Why should apologies on behalf of perpetrators of ecclesiastical abuse be any more acceptable?

Specious arguments were deployed about it not being possible to act in both a judicial and a pastoral manner. However, any parent or schoolteacher knows that when a child misbehaves, you need to respond with both discipline and love – indeed, this is how Jesus of Nazareth treated his own disciples.

No surprise, then, that survivors coming forward about clerical sexual abuse were not generally offered meaningful support, pastoral or otherwise, but directed to the CDM. Most refused to use the CDM, with good reason. Research shows that well over 96% of those making allegations of clerical sexual abuse are truthful. However, investigations collapse due to 'insufficient evidence' and if a CDM does go forward, the evidentiary standards applied would fail to deliver guilty verdicts in almost all cases. The perpetrator almost always 'wins', takes satisfaction in seeing how he and the Church have damaged his target and can claim vindication. Retaliation may then be taken by the perpetrator and/or by the Church against the complainant.

The Church went on to produce a series of safeguarding policy documents. Safeguarding was presented as being of paramount importance, and the stated policies, if incomplete, were at least fair. However, some two thousand survivors reported that responses by the Church were more harmful than the original sexual abuse. The Church's own policies were not being followed. It turned out that they were merely non-binding, advisory guidance.

What Bishop Paul Butler referred to as 're-abuse' would more accurately be called 'institutional grooming and abuse'.

The CDM was amended and from 1 October 2016, failure to comply with House of Bishops' safeguarding guidance became a disciplinary offence. The Independent Inquiry into Child Sexual Abuse (IICSA) held hearings into safeguarding failures in the Church of England in March 2018, when the lead bishop for safeguarding in the House of Bishops was asked whether the 'due regard' provision had been applied. He replied, 'I don't know that with any certainty.' It seems as if nothing has actually changed. What good is law if it's not enforced?

Things are changing fast at the moment, particularly since the IICSA hearings publicly exposed so much about the ill treatment of survivors by the Church. However, even if survivors are treated better in future, there is a very substantial backlog of cases that the Church needs to address and remediate.

The Church has recently put into place a very large-scale training programme explaining safeguarding policies and procedures, and emphasising the seriousness of abuse. Trainees are instructed that abuse is complex and sensitive and are advised to direct matters to their diocesan safeguarding team, who will 'take care of it for you'.

Survivors are seen as a threat and treated as potential litigants. Safeguarding officers and administrative staff see it as their job to protect bishops from having to deal with survivors and to minimise liability to the diocese.

Survivors seeking a meeting to disclose what happened can be kept waiting for many months, a year or more before seeing someone in authority who could investigate and take action – but few get that far. After initial contact with a safeguarding office, the staff would spend more time explaining how 'we are very busy' than in setting a date for a meeting, and employ a wide range of techniques to put off the survivor in their struggle to be heard.

If a meeting with a safeguarding officer does take place, survivors may hear that, contrary to the promises made in the institutional grooming stage, 'we don't know anyone who could provide pastoral support' and 'we don't have a list of counsellors'. Survivors are advised that they have the right to use the CDM, but are also told that 'we can't refer you to a lawyer'.

Perpetrators may be offered legal aid by the Church but complainants are not eligible. It is clear that the Church would like survivors to just shut up and go away.

Safeguarding staff know that disclosures of child abuse need to be reported to the police – and that the Church need take no further meaningful action unless there has been a conviction. In one diocese, it took 44 years of police referrals before a known clerical paedophile was convicted, whereupon the bishop removed the now retired priest's permission to officiate. If it's about the abuse of vulnerable adults, where the legal position is complex, the matter is usually left with the survivor, who is blamed for not being willing and able to cooperate with the Church. Hardly surprising, given C of E policy to put the re-abusive diocese in charge of their cases. This is the institutional equivalent to offering the survivor 'informed pastoral care and support' from the priest who abused them.

Church safeguarding officers know at some level that mistreating vulnerable survivors is disempowering, if not incapacitating or even re-traumatising. However, they make sure to stay just on the right side of the procedural line, knowing that even if they slip up, the survivor has no realistic chance of challenging their mistreatment successfully. The safeguarding staff can shrug their shoulders when asked why survivors didn't accept the 'help' being offered and lost trust in the Church.

Those survivors who persist in seeking to have the matter investigated by the Church and for the perpetrator to be held to account may encounter ever more officious, manipulative and threatening behaviour. Further persistence in seeking justice from the Church can lead to retaliation that can be devastating and even life threatening. The costs to survivors in terms of paying for therapy or counselling, damage to health, distress, ruined relationships, lost income etc. mount as the years go by.

The National Church has conducted large-scale safeguarding exercises such as the Past Cases Review (PCR), but this did not include input from survivors – by design – ostensibly to minimise distress to survivors. And when the PCR was itself reviewed in 2017–2018, it was extraordinary that the Independent Scrutiny Team (IST) also omitted survivor input, presumably to avoid 'mission creep'. Nevertheless, the IST found that improvement was needed in the Church's responses to survivors of abuse by clergy and church officials. However, not being based on primary research, this is under-evidenced assertion and can easily be ignored.

The terms of reference for a major audit of diocesan safeguarding arrangements by the Social Care Institute for Excellence (SCIE) also omitted survivors. The SCIE auditors encountered only one survivor in all 42 dioceses in England – myself – and I got in under the radar as a member of a diocesan safeguarding panel.

Meanwhile, ecclesiastical abuse survivors began resorting to the blogosphere to put their side of the story across, joining survivors of abuse in other settings. The #MeToo movement grew rapidly from late 2017. Society is growing increasingly intolerant of abuse, including institutional abuse.

The IICSA hearings in March 2018 seem to have been a watershed for the Church, as bishops heard detailed evidence from survivors of ecclesiastical abuse in the Diocese of Chichester, apparently for the first time.

In 2018, SCIE began a small add-on research project to the diocesan safeguarding audit looking into how responses from the Church to survivors and those needing help to keep safe can be improved. Preliminary results of a survey of survivors and others at risk of harm were presented at General Synod in July 2018. However, if prior experience of independent safeguarding reviews is anything to go by, recommendations arising from this research may not be accepted by the Church, or perhaps nominally accepted but ignored in practice.

The Church of England's safeguarding policies are not working. They are broken, and along with them, the Church itself is broken. When one member of the body of Christ is harmed, the entire Church is wounded.

Church of England safeguarding policy stands at a crossroads. Continuing in the same direction would lead to catastrophe as it has for other churches around the world. The Church must change direction if its brokenness is not to be its undoing.

Consider the following choices:

Route 1: Keep going with centralised management of safeguarding practice, including (a) uncritical safeguarding training that does not take into account the causes of abuse or how to address them; (b) continue to commission reviews and audits that omit input from survivors; and (c) continue generating ever more convoluted structures, policies, procedures and guidance whilst still avoiding holding perpetrators of ecclesiastical abuse to account. Passively await 'culture change'.

Route 2: Commission a comprehensive, independent evaluation of the actual conduct and impacts of safeguarding in the Church of England, covering church leaders, safeguarding officers, perpetrators, congregations and survivors, and a budgetary analysis. Implement its recommendations.

Route 3: Engage in a widespread process of learning about ecclesiastical abuse in all corners of the Church, from the causes of pastoral failures by individual priests to contributory social factors such as a sense of entitlement amongst the elite in English society. Once ecclesiastical abuse is better understood, the Church will be better equipped to respond constructively to survivors, to work with perpetrators and traumatised congregations, and to prevent (re-)abuse from occurring.

Route 4: Adopt policies and practices currently used in the health sector to protect patient safety. Embed professional ethics into the ecclesiastical culture as it is done in medicine. There should be annual assessments of fitness to practice as in the NHS. When there are safeguarding failures, the Church should investigate and deal with specific cases, much as the General Medical Council takes responsibility for breaches in medical professionalism.

Route 5: Adopt practices applied to the police and the press. Set up an Independent Ecclesiastical Complaints Commission that could issue binding rulings, which may involve conferring greater powers to the police and/or other statutory bodies.

Route 6: Penalise failures of 'due regard' to House of Bishops safeguarding guidance. Hold perpetrators of ecclesiastical abuse to account by whatever means necessary to achieve justice and to protect other vulnerable people from harm. Accept full responsibility for compensating those harmed by (re-)abuse directly, without subjecting survivors to legal or civil proceedings or insurance protocols which are almost as traumatising – saving considerable amounts of time, trouble and cost to the Church as well as to the survivors.

Route 7: Focus on survivors and their needs, listening to them as a matter of priority. As Jesus asked Bartimaeus after attempts at silencing him had failed, ask survivors, "What is it that you would like me to do for you?" Take the initiative, inviting survivors to meet over a cuppa tea whether down the corner cafe or at the House of Lords. Offer pastoral, liturgical and sacramental ministry, including services and retreats specifically devoted to healing from abuse.

While ensuring that their personal privacy is respected, invite survivors to participate in church music, Messy Church, away days and other parish activities.

Whatever route is followed, it should be for the sake of all those who are affected by ecclesiastical abuse, from "the least of these" – the victims and survivors – to families, chaplaincies, congregations and church leaders. All need healing.

Being the Church of England, it is likely that different individuals and parts of the institution will follow different routes at different rates.

But hang on a minute. What is the destination to which these routes should lead?

The answer should be obvious. The journey is not to a destination but a Way. It is a pilgrimage into the Kingdom of God.

Christianity itself contains everything that is needed to respond to sin, including clerical and institutional grooming and abuse. The

Church needs to follow Jesus of Nazareth, whose radical challenge to the religious authorities of his day may have led to his execution – but he died so that we should not have to die.

Facile or convoluted theological approaches need to be challenged, such as misplaced pressure on survivors to rid themselves of the burden of abuse by putting it down and forgiving those who have (re-) abused them.

Reconciliation is only possible if those responsible for ecclesiastical abuse confess what they have done, express true remorse and explain how they aim to set things right. Only then can they reasonably be forgiven by survivors – and by God.

The real solution to the ecclesiastical abuse crisis is pastoral: 'tough love' applied to perpetrators through pastoral supervision (including legal sanctions if the perpetrator is unrepentant) – and unconditional ministry to survivors. Structures, policies, procedures and guidance should be secondary to observing God's two great commandments. It is far more important to understand the causes of abuse, to listen to and to provide pastoral support for survivors, and to use informed pastoral interventions with perpetrators and traumatised congregations. What is most needed is highly professional, Christian ministry.

Only by following the Way of Jesus may the broken body of Christ be healed.

Dr Josephine Anne Stein *is an independent researcher, policy analyst, and survivor of ecclesiastical abuse.*

Chapter 32

The Crisis of The Hierarchy

Alan Wilson

"The only monkeys who think their bottoms aren't red are the ones at the top of the tree." – Indian Proverb.

When I was ordained in the late 1970s there were still a few traditional country parsons around. There was an old man in our deanery who used to ride around his village on a white horse, clipping kiddies round the ear if they dared to scrump apples from the rectory orchard.

There was an eccentric but rather authoritarian clergyman nearby whom nobody could understand. He was known to his wedding couples as "Old Snuffy" because he often took snuff and sneezed uncontrollably during interviews with young people.

Liturgically and in other ways, the clergy ruled the roost. As a young curate I went to take the service in a small rural parish and was asked by a verger, "what are your peculiarities, sir?" I thought of Isaac Watts' line about every creature rising to bring "Peculiar offerings to their King." I wasn't aware of having any peculiarities, or needing to. I asked him what his were, and he was nonplussed.

All clergy, in his experience, had peculiarities, he said. Worship was nothing much to do with the people in the pews, and everything to do with the personal proclivities of clergy, many of whom forced on the congregations committed to their charge, with a rod of iron, their own tastes, learning, and obsessions.

There was a generally relaxed standard of accountability among clergy. Many saw themselves as lords of all they surveyed. A Methodist colleague with whom I worked in the prison service was taken, the day after his induction, into the high street of a West Country market town by the Anglican rector. The rector waved his arm with an expansive gesture towards the crowds milling around and said, by way of welcome, "I hope you will be very happy here, but what you will have to remember is that these people are all mine!"

In those far-off days there was a tremendous tolerance of clerical eccentricity, and much forbearance towards it. This eccentricity could take the form of obsessional interest in model railways, beekeeping, or detective novels. It was always deferred to unquestioningly.

Appointments to posts were generally made by word of mouth on the basis of personal recommendation, or sometimes dinner in a London gentlemen's club, surrounded by an aura of secrecy and jobbing. Some clergy had private means, but even for those who did not there was still an aura of upper class effortless superiority, when they attended the summer fete in high collar and linen jacket.

One archdeacon's wife famously told an audience of young clergy wives in my early days, "The clerical profession is not well paid, and those of you who have worked will find little time for such things because your calling is to support your husband in and about the parish. But vicarage life has its compensations — you do get the pick of the jumble."

Changes in society's makeup and expectations, the ordination of women, the Church's general decline in numbers and influence, have put paid to the not-so-good old ways.

Socially, operationally, liturgically and theologically, thank God all that nonsense is over. Non-episcopal clergy no longer enjoy the kinds of freehold they once they did; not in the same way, anyway. Vicars have had to reinvent themselves in the past fifty years. They couldn't get away with the old nonsense any more.

There would be nobody left in church if they were silly enough to try.

When massive social change happens there are always early adopters, keen to try out new possibilities. One thing thousands of pages of the Independent Inquiry into Child Sexual Abuse (IICSA) evidence has revealed about the Church of England in the early twenty-first century – to anyone with the patience to read it – is the large amount of fudge, muddle, mendacity and bodge in the work of its most senior echelons.

There, grinning out of the tree like the Cheshire Cat's smile, that outlasted the animal itself, are just about the only clergy left who still seem lost in wonder love and joy about themselves. They no longer believe something to be true, worthwhile or allowable simply because they said it or did it. The only group still running on the old operating system is the bishops.

Thus it can be no surprise that IICSA evidence says power has been shoddily and unaccountably exercised in dense fog, in what many senior leaders of the Church took at the time to be a generally consequence-free environment. If any good can come out of the squirm-making evidence of IICSA, it will be the end of much episcopal and para-episcopal bloody nonsense.

This is not to say bishops and senior clergy are generally bad people. My experience is quite the reverse. As the people they are, I find them often thoughtful, reflective, engaging, and conscientious. But as a corporate entity, something in the system has turned senior bishops into good people who do bad things without realising how awful they are. The whole has ended up as very much less than the sum of the parts.

So what is the hierarchy good for? By and large two purposes.

One is a matter of what in other contexts would be called quality assurance. The episkopos of the ancient city was, among other things, the inspector of drains. His job was to keep the waters flowing cleanly into the drains, and swiftly down the sewers. For bishops this function often means maintaining the Church structure so as to restrain bullies. Bishops are to care for justice, for that is the first claim of love. They are to bring the resources of Scripture, Christian experience and reason to bear on contemporary conundra and guide with wisdom and discretion; not as defenders of their own privileged Ecclesiastical Verdun ("none shall pass"), but as animators of a living and breathing tradition that spreads and passes itself on virally, and with integrity.

Secondly, bishops embody in every generation the critical tension between Jesus and the Pharisees. In justice to the Pharisees it needs to be said that they included many good people like Nicodemus and Gamaliel. Other professional guardians of the sacred also received a consistent tongue-lashing from Jesus, including scribes, doctors of the law, and temple sales staff. An important function of the principal leaders in any Church is to keep it focused on following Jesus Christ.

When Churches fail to maintain this focus, they very soon end up following Caiaphas instead. By washing the feet of his disciples Jesus laid down a principle that the acid test of a church is not how any people go, or how good they feel when they do, but how power is used among them.

Jesus was clear about the issues here. When his disciples saw exalted professional guardians of the Sacred sitting in the seat of Moses, they were to do as the leaders said, not as they did. They were to beware the leaven of the Pharisees, with its pernicious and powerful tendency to take over religious institutions and make them self-regarding, self serving, enjoying a liberty St Peter graphically called, "a cloak of maliciousness."

To help his disciples avoid the leaven of the Pharisees, Jesus clearly articulated amber light characteristics to watch out for in religious leaders. Do they scour land and sea for converts to make like themselves, assessed for numbers not quality of life ? Do they lay burdens on others that they would never care to bear? Do they love praying on the street corners and having best places of honour? Are they obsessional about keeping the outside of the cup clean, whilst ignoring the rot inside? Do people defer to them, but ignore them, like whitewashed tombs you can walk over without even noticing they're there? Do they do their business at night? Do they think, on the whole, it is better for the individual to be sacrificed than the holy place compromised? Are they so absorbed in their religious duties and learning that they cannot see the broken victim in the road, let alone divert from their planned course to help?

These are painfully searching questions. Jesus gave them to his disciples because they matter desperately. The truth of the Church is not that it is always right. No serious student of church history could suppose anything so false. Its truth arises from the way in which, in every generation, God has laid down through the Church a clear choice between the way of Christ and way of Caiaphas. Many people today do not want to join the Church of England not because they are secularised in an anti-God way, but because they can see through the paper-thin hypocrisy and self-serving of the elites who run the Church as their own personal fiefdom.

Where do bishops fit into this scenario? It might seem tempting to ditch the whole idea of hierarchy, but quite apart from giving nobody to complain to, historical experience of communities that have done this has not been promising. Far from producing a paradisal order of equality, the usual results have been tyranny or chaos. Back in the 1980s, Heavy Shepherding, with all its abusive baggage, used to be the speciality of churches that boasted proudly that they had no hierarchical structure. Experience says that churches that pretend they have no hierarchy are usually only saying that their hierarchy is hidden. Somebody has to take on the job of constraining bullies and keeping the drains running in this particular iteration of the unfolding Christian tradition, and it might as well be bishops under that title as any other.

The duty of bishops, in this sense, is to be Nicodemus-type Pharisees, open to the wind of the Spirit blowing where it will. Or they could be Gamaliel-type Pharisees, leaving judgment and the future to

God's wisdom beyond their control. Some could even be radical prophetic Paul-type Pharisees, open to radical conversion and deep experience of grace. Following Jesus Christ cannot be squared, however, with being a Caiaphas-type Pharisee — checkboxing, anxious for the institution, defensive, scapegoating, secretive.

The way in which bishops occupy their formally Pharisaic position and exercise its functions is crucial. It can be very healing if they hold a formally Pharisaic position and discharge their responsibilities in truthful, accountable and transparent ways. It disinfects the whole notion of hierarchy and puts it at the service of the entire community.

If, however, the way they occupy their place demonstrates nothing more than the stale old Pharisee games that Jesus excoriated, the Church will have to fix around the problem in spite of, not aided by, its senior leaders, by treating them as a roundabout.

The old Scots Covenanters rejected episcopacy because of the way it had been exercised in their experience— not episcopacy in the technical sense (for they were not anarchists) but what they called Prelacy. This was the capricious and opaque use of power for self-serving ends. Whatever its supporting force of habit or history, whatever the punters are prepared to allow hierarchs to get away with, it is a stain on any Christian community.

If the bishops of the Church of England are to encompass the same cultural reinvention of their ministry that local clergy have had to in the past 40 years, this will involve turning from panicky elitist prelacy to a genuine form of servant oversight.

I am fairly sure that many, probably most, bishops I know would actually like that personally. It would release their gifts and set them free to be themselves.

There's another paradox in the IICSA evidence however. One of its real puzzles has been to hear a parade of senior ecclesiastics, people who were thought to be responsible and running the entire show, declaring that actually they have no power to do anything and the whole mess is somehow nothing to do with them. If not them, Basil Fawlty might ask, to whom might we look for responsibility? Dennis Compton?

Given the personal qualities of the people concerned I have no idea why the Church of England has made such a hash of safeguarding; in so many contexts, and at so senior a level, and for so many years, but it has. I could say I feel betrayed by people I trusted, but anything I say along those lines is dwarfed by the experience of hundreds, possibly thousands of ordinary survivors of abuse who have been betrayed by the complicity, bungling, mendacity and *folie de grandeur* of the monkeys at the top of the tree.

The critical situation in which we find ourselves, if we have any conscience, drives me back to the basics.

I was once asked to appear at a military dinner in my episcopal regalia. "Yes, of course," I said, "but what do you want me to do?"

"Do?" said the Colonel. "I don't want you to do anything. The purpose of a bishop at a function like this is to add tone. Like cavalry in the age of mechanised warfare."

Beyond this, what are bishops for? What could they be?

The ordinal is perfectly straightforward. "With the Shepherd's love, they are to be merciful, but with firmness; to minister discipline, but with compassion. They are to have a special care for the poor, the outcast and those who are in need."

That's why every bishop is asked at their ordination: "Will you be gentle and merciful for Christ's sake to those who are in need, and speak for those who have no other to speak for them?"

Experience of working with survivors of abuse in the Church has shown me that Church of England bishops have rather underperformed in this duty. Renewal of the episcopate awaits, as the behaviours and attitudes of what used to be called the "Inferior Clergy" has had to be renewed since the 1960s.

It's about time, surely, we bishops stopped making pathetic excuses, blaming everybody else for the mess, hiding behind the sofa and phoning the registrar, being self-important busy bunnies, and handwringing.

This is not about preventing bishops from being bishops. It's about enabling them to fulfil their calling in a much less shoddy, elitist way. It's about time we bishops stopped handwringing and started doing our job properly. To do this we must stop trying to run new software on an obsolete operating system (what Jesus called trying to store new wine in old wineskins).

The state of affairs revealed by IICSA calls for bishops to accomplish in our order what priests have already had to do in theirs, years ago – transform a culture of secrecy, effortless superiority and neurotic *folie de grandeur* into one of openness, service, and accountability. Why not?

Alan Wilson *is Bishop of Buckingham.*

Chapter 33

Violence in the Mind of God

Linda Woodhead

What do we know
But that we face
One another in this place.
– William Butler Yeats

There is a flurry of activity around safeguarding in the Church of England at the moment, and much reassurance that the abuse crisis is under control. I don't believe it, because I see no evidence of any attempt to look searchingly at every aspect of Church life to find what has gone wrong and put it right. It's as if abuse and safeguarding exists in one compartment, hermetically sealed from the others. When it comes to the structure and hierarchy of the Church, the accountability of bishops, clerical training, the whole paraphernalia of 'renewal and reform', it seems to be business as usual. Theology cannot be immune from this necessary self-examination and reconstruction, because it is the Church's ultimate source of inspiration and its court of appeal. The issue of what this might involve is what concerns me here.

The obvious place to start is with God. It won't be the first time people have asked whether there is a link between images of God in Bible and tradition and violence – especially violence against women and children. Two examples with lasting power spring to mind. In the 1980s the biblical scholar Phyllis Trible drew attention to 'texts of terror' in the scriptures (in her book of that title), including Abraham's near sacrifice of his child at God's command, and Jephthah's actual sacrifice of his. And in *Spare the Child* the historian Philip Greven (1990) traced how Biblical commandments to discipline children violently have shaped Protestant cultures down to the modern period.

Trible and Greven leave no doubt that the texts they deal with are not distortions of Bible and tradition; they are part of it. However blasphemous it may sound, an urgent question that must be asked in the shadow of the abuse scandal is how the Christian God may have been presented as a predatory and abusive figure, and given the blessing of 'orthodoxy'.

Abuse is primarily about the exercise of dominating and destroying power; if it includes sex – as it often does – it does so as a tool of bodily and emotional domination. There is an uncomfortable parallel here with how the Church has presented God as a supreme, dominating and discipling power that must be obeyed, and with its obsession with controlling the sex lives of its followers.

But abuse involves more than acts of bodily domination. There is often careful and long-term preparation ('grooming') and an ongoing, confusing, and infantilising relationship between abuser and abused. Worryingly, there are theological parallels here as well. God knows what is best for his children. Though his commands may seem arbitrary, it is a privilege to be singled out by him. He demands the total surrender of body and soul. The preparation may be long and hard, and should start as a child. The will must be broken. The worst sin according to much Christian teaching since Augustine is pride (not violence) – rebellion against God. Only when individuals confess their sinfulness, are humiliated and broken, can they be saved. Then will God take them in his arms and fill them with his Spirit. Sin, pride and rebellion can creep back in, so the faithful must remain vigilant and loyal to God and his deputies, resistant to the 'unorthodox' voices that would lure them away.

It may be objected that this view is no longer current, though it was certainly the one I was raised with, and plenty of other girls my age. Stephen Bernard, younger than me, encountered it more recently in the Catholic Church. He says of Canon Fogarty, his serial abuser, that:

> [H]e managed to make a spiritual deed of a physical one. There are two ways of saying the word confessor in English, and both of them mean rape to me. The man to whom one confesses and the act of confession, each and both are contained in that one word: confessor, rape. (Paper Cuts, 2018)

In recent exposures of abuse in the Church of England, we have learned that some of its clerical abusers drew directly on this dominating, predatory understanding of God. It was essential to their 'work'. Coming from different ends of the theological spectrum, both the conservative evangelical John Smyth and the Anglo-Catholic monk Bishop Peter Ball presented themselves as spiritual mentors for specially chosen young men. Smyth drew on biblical texts about fathers disciplining their sons, while Ball also used Franciscan spirituality. When they made their victims strip and be beaten, they explained that humiliation was a sign of obedience to God, a penance and a prophylactic for sin. Their abuse went deep into the soul as well as they body of their victims, leaving ineradicable damage.

Although predators like Smyth and Ball are rare, what's concerning is the extent to which they were found credible, even admirable, by many Christians around them, even after their activities were exposed. Instead of reporting him to the police, for example, Smyth's supporters sent him abroad; some continued to fund his 'ministry' in Zimbabwe and then South Africa (where he resided until his death in August 2018). Ball's supporters included at least ten brother bishops to whom disclosures of abuse were made, none of whom reported him. Prominent amongst Ball's supporters was the Archbishop of Canterbury, George Carey, and Charles, Prince of Wales. Both smeared victims as malicious troublemakers and, even after Ball was cautioned by police, remained convinced he was a remarkable spiritual leader who should be rehabilitated as quickly as possible. He chimed with their theological understanding.

Still, it may be claimed that the fearful, dark and demanding Father God has been replaced in most churches today by a 'lighter' image of God as a loving and beneficent father and companion, and Jesus as a personal saviour and friend. I accept this. The influence of both liberal theology and charismatic renewal, and possibly the ministry of more women, has pushed in this direction. This is a God who doesn't seek to master and humiliate his followers but comes to them in self-giving love and asks for the same in return, freely given. Some speak of a 'kenotic' God, who creates by withdrawing and making space for the creation, enabling our very existence. He is said to love us so much that he sacrifices his only Son.

Can we be sure, however, that even this kenotic view has freed itself from the old idea of a zero-sum equation between God and humans, such that one must decrease for the other to increase? There is still much talk of God as a 'Father', and of his majesty, kingliness and lordship in charismatic circles. There is still 'shepherding', and 'discipling', and charismatic male leaders. Has the C of E truly abandoned an understanding of clergy deputising for the Father and Jesus as 'fathers', 'shepherds', or confessors able to absolve? Has the interpretation of Jesus's execution as a foreordained and once-for-all sacrificial offering to God demanding human surrender been seriously re-examined in the light of abuse?

Even if we believe that the God of fear and submission is truly in abeyance, the God of light and love brings its own dangers. The C of E today promotes itself with positive images. Its publicity materials show shiny, happy Christians living fulfilled lives in the context of loving and supportive Christian 'families', both biological and ecclesial. 'See how these Christians love each other', is the message, and love is interpreted as 'unity' at all costs. It is joined with the imperative of 'mission', interpreted as bringing more people to church. The Church is being portrayed as a beacon of light and love in a darkening world.

The danger here is idealisation. The pressure to concentrate on points of brightness and cover over the darkness becomes very great. This can mean turning a blind eye to abusive practices and individuals. A striking example is the Past Cases Review (PCR) undertaken under Rowan William's leadership.

Presented as an attempt to clean up the Church's act by trawling through 30,000 clergy files to make sure there was no evidence of abuse not followed up, it turned into an exercise in whitewash that revealed only thirteen such cases in the whole Church. Ironically, it is the derided 'secular' society in the shape of Independent Inquiry into Child Sexual Abuse that has had to shine a light in the dark places of the Church.

Idealisation confuses being Christian, and being Church, with being happy and good. A kind of perfectionism takes over – the C of E as Camelot. On this understanding, the Church already possesses the Truth and is a guardian of 'Orthodoxy', its only task being to proclaim it more energetically. What's needed is 'teaching', not soul-searching. Such a Church can have nothing to learn from outside, or from lay experts, and must try to contain and conceal abuses. It becomes impossible to admit to failures and incompetence, lest the whole edifice come crashing down.

This idealisation of faith also makes it harder for individuals and congregations to examine their demons. The only option for those who claim a special relationship with the God of light and love is to cast them out and become a child of light. A friend of mine once attended a service in a Pentecostal church in which a symbolic river of baptism was traced on the floor, and the congregation invited to cross over it and be washed clean of their demons. My friend refused on the grounds that she had lived so long with hers she wouldn't know what to do without them. She was making a serious theological point, perhaps the same one as the parable of the Gadarene swine. We can be honest about our demons, even playful and exploratory with them, 'testing the spirits' to know which are of God. We can make peace with some, and concentrate our efforts on controlling others. Or we can try to banish them completely, and find that we end up in a worse state.

When moral standards are made absolute, and consequences of transgression unspeakable, the result is often not goodness, but secrecy. Bad things breed in the dark. Holding clergy to higher standards than laity has been shown to be a factor in abuse in the Catholic Church, and the C of E does exactly the same – in its teaching document *Issues in Human Sexuality*, for example. The danger is that clergy interpret a personal lapse as the crossing of a threshold from which there is no recovery. They may enter a dark, secret, and exciting place. A 'light' side is on show in public, a dark one in private. The darkness may become a realm of freedom and rebellion, and issues that could have been sorted out with a bit of honesty and common sense become dangerous.

Ethical and spiritual life is a process, not an ontological state of sin or sanctity. To say blithely that 'we are all sinners' is a dangerous way of denying shades of grey and ducking the demanding process of making moral discernments between them. It's as evasive as the idea that Christians must forgive anything at the drop of a hat and move on. The Independent Inquiry into Child Sexual Abuse was told that the Rev Gordon Rideout, sentenced to ten years' imprisonment for 36 separate sex offences against 16 different children 'took the view that he had been forgiven by God, his slate was therefore wiped clean ... as if the abuse hadn't happened.'

Underlying some of this is the idea that all that really matters is my personal relationship with God, which is separate from my relation with the world. If God forgives me, that's all that matters. Faith becomes a transaction between self and God, not part of the ongoing business of living better in a web of interactions and mutual dependencies. God is then a get-out clause from living a responsible life in the world, rather than an inspiration to live fully and well.

When the 'Church of England' is true to its name, it doesn't proclaim itself a universal Church but a Church bound up with a particular, limited, and fallible nation and culture. That's a much better starting point for dealing honestly with its failings. An honest examination of the role of theology must take place in an open conversation with others, including public enquiries and people the Church has abused. Not surprisingly, some these survivors have thought long and hard about their faith in exactly the way I am commending here. They must help in the long but vital task of creating post-abusive theologies, if the Church is to be saved.

Linda Woodhead MBE is Professor of the Sociology of Religion in the Department of Politics, Philosophy and Religion at Lancaster University.

Contributors

Some authors have chosen to remain anonymous for personal or security reasons.

Anne is an Anglican priest.

Rupert Bursell QC is an Anglican priest and abuse survivor. He has served as a judge and as chancellor of several dioceses. In 2018 he was awarded the Canterbury Cross, "for his contribution to the understanding and application of ecclesiastical law in the Church of England."

Miryam Clough is the author of *Shame, the Church, and the Regulation of Female Sexuality* (Routledge, 2017).

Natalie Collins is a Gender Justice Specialist working to enable individuals and organisations to prevent and respond to male violence against women. She has created the DAY Programme for young people, and the Own My Life course for women; she organises Project 3:28; and co-founded the UK Christian Feminist Network. Natalie blogs and tweets as 'God Loves Women' and is the author of *Gender Aware Youth Practice* (Grove Booklets) and *Out Of Control: couples, conflict and the capacity for change* (SPCK, 2019).

Ian Elliott is an independent safeguarding consultant that has worked across five continents and with many Churches. He is a professional social worker with over forty years of experience gained within statutory child protection services and within voluntary bodies.

Janet Fife was one of the first women to be ordained in the Church of England. She is a writer and survivor and has a research degree in the pastoral care of survivors. She is disabled.

Gilo is a survivor, hymn-writer, and outsider theologian.

Graham is a survivor of the Iwerne camps and John Smyth.

Andrew Graystone is a theologian and writer. As a journalist he broke the story of the abuse by John Smyth QC in the Iwerne network and in Africa. He continues to advocate for all victims of abuse.

David Greenwood is Head of Child Abuse at Switalskis Solicitors.

Rosie Harper is Vicar of Great Missenden and Chaplain to the Bishop of Buckingham.

Adrian Hilton is a theologian, political philosopher, educationalist and author. He lectures in the UK and the US.

Peter Hitchens is an author and columnist for the Mail on Sunday.

Cliff James is a writer and poet.

Jo Kind is a survivor, a MACSAS (Ministers and Clergy Sexual Abuse Survivors) committee member, and a volunteers support worker.

Janet Lord works in a university in the North West of England. She previously trained as a tax inspector.

Matthew is a survivor of sexual abuse.

Jayne Ozanne is a survivor of abuse, and a member of the Church of England's General Synod. She has previously been a member of the Archbishops' Council. She is founder and Director of the Ozanne Foundation.

Stephen Parsons is a retired Anglican priest who lives in the Diocese of Carlisle. He has studied the issue of church abuse since the mid-90s and edits a blog, www.survivivgchurch.org.

Carrie Pemberton Ford, author, speaker, academic and priest, is the Executive Director for CCARHT, a counter human trafficking think tank, based in Cambridge, working inter-disciplinarily across the University. www.ccarht.org. She was the first ordained clergywoman to be appointed to Government Office as a Woman's National Commissioner in 2004, and was a founder member of the National Executive of WATCH (Women and the Church).

Martyn Percy is Dean of Christ Church, Oxford, and Vice President of Modern Church.

Christina Rees CBE is a writer, broadcaster, speaker, preacher and practical theologian working primarily with issues of women and religion and contemporary Christian spirituality. She was a member of General Synod for 25 years and a founder member of the Archbishops' Council.

Graham Sawyer is an Anglican priest and a survivor.

Richard Scorer is Head of Abuse Law at Slater and Gordon and represents victims and survivors at Independent Inquiry into Child Sexual Abuse (IICSA). He is Vice President of the National Secular Society (NSS).

Martin Sewell is a member of General Synod for the Rochester Diocese and a retired Child Protection Solicitor.

Josephine Anne Stein is an independent researcher, policy analyst, and survivor of ecclesiastical abuse.

Alan Wilson is Bishop of Buckingham.

Linda Woodhead MBE is Professor of the Sociology of Religion in the Department of Politics, Philosophy and Religion at Lancaster University.

Acknowledgements

The publication of this book has been made possible by the generous contributions of donors to our crowd-funding campaign last year. We would like to extend our heartfelt thanks to them.

Anonymous
Stephen Parsons
Anonymous
Alan T L Wilson
Anonymous
Helen King
Miranda Threlfall-
    Holmes
Nicholas Elder
Mandy Barbante
Peter Owen
Jan Ashton
Ian Elliott
Lisa Perkins
Jan
Anonymous
Anonymous
Christian Hernandez
Richard Scorer
Deirdre McCormack
Rosie Harper
Anonymous
Carolyn Graham
Anonymous
Anonymous
Anne Foreman
Samuel Austin
David Rhodes

Simon Sarmiento
Janet Lord
Anonymous
Anonymous
Lisa Battye
Neil Patterson
Anonymous
Bernard Silverman
Jeremy Trew
Alistair McBay
Anonymous
Anonymous
David Craig
Andrew McMullon
Rev Graham
    Hamilton
Father Gareth Jones
Tim Hind
Jonathan Young
Charles Clapham
Martyn Percy
David Lamming
Anonymous
Berkeley Zych
Roy Humphrey
Anonymous
Jennifer Humphreys
Hugh Constant

Roy Parsons
Anonymous
Anthony Archer
John Tasker
Adam Leigh
    Shepherd
Robert Beaver
John Duncan
Mark Russell
Fr. Michael Robinson
Anonymous
Anonymous
Joyce Jones
Anonymous
Jack Belloli
James Hollingsworth
Bishop of Salisbury
Katherine Hedderly
Julie Conalty
Laurence Gamlen
Sharon Copestake
Rev'd Rosie Bates
Rachel Mann
Karen Gorham
Andrew Dotchin
Christopher Jones
Anonymous
Alison Bird

Anonymous
Stephen Evans
Gordon Lynch
Anonymous
Margaret Bannister
Anonymous
Catherine Davies
Christine Alison E
   Kaan
Nigel and Imogen
   Walsh

Colin Bradley
Mx Ljós Greenleaf
Margherita Watt
Peppy Ulyett
Patricia Lyon
Rt Rev'd Dr Gavin
   Ashenden
Liz Martin
Anonymous
Anonymous
Rachel Nicholls

Bryan Kerr
Ruth Tattum
Anonymous
Martin Sewell
Joey Murréll
David Mason
Christopher Perry

We are grateful also to Simon Barrow and Bob Carling of Ekklesia, and other assistants on legal, technical and design issues, for enabling this publication. We thankfully acknowledge Kevin Mayhew for reproduction of the poem 'The Cheerful Hymn', by Lucy Berry.

About MACSAS

MACSAS (Minister and Clergy Sexual Abuse Survivors) is a support group for women and men from Christian backgrounds who have been sexually abused by Ministers or Clergy, as children or as adults. We support both survivors who have remained within their Christian communities and for those who have left.

Dr Margaret Kennedy founded MACSAS in the late 1990s, following requests from clergy abuse survivors who attended Christian Survivors of Sexual Abuse (CSSA), which she also founded in 1989.

All who work for MACSAS are volunteers, who themselves are survivors. Helpline workers are trained and certified to undertake helpline duties.

More information here: https://www.macsas.org.uk/index.html

Any profits from this book and the fundraising that enabled it, after costs have been covered, will go to support the work of MACSAS and towards the cost of a possible conference and related activity associated with this book.

About Ekklesia

Ekklesia is an independent network providing 'thought space' for exploring the impact of ethics and beliefs in the areas of public and social policy.

We want to encourage transformative local engagement with global issues – not least among moral communities (churches and other groups) who see themselves as being firmly committed to people at the margins.

Our operational values are those of social justice, inclusion, nonviolence, environmental action, participative democracy and creative exchange among those of different convictions (religious or otherwise).

Ekklesia is active in promoting – alongside others – new models of mutual economy, conflict transformation, peacemaking, social power, restorative justice, citizen action and truth-telling in public life. This means moving beyond 'top-down', colonial approaches to politics, economics and beliefs.

While strongly influenced by the Peace Churches and grassroots movements for social change, Ekklesia is keen to work with people of many backgrounds who share common principles and approaches.

Ekklesia's reports, news analysis and commentary can be accessed via our website (www.ekklesia.co.uk) on Twitter (Ekklesia_co_uk) and on Facebook (www.facebook.com/ekklesiathinktank/).